The Exotic and the Mundane by Joyce Dickens
Published by UPTRN
PO Box 401
Laporte, CO 80535
www.UPTRN.com

Joyce@LearningToTravel.com

www.LearningToTravel.com

Cover by Lotus Designs.
Cover Image by Daryle Dickens

First Edition

The Exotic & the Mundane
Joyce Dickens

Contents

Prologue - Why I decided to write a book 5

1. How we came to take our "trip of a lifetime." 7

2. Leaving Home 13

3. Sayulita, Mexico (Days 1 to 29) 19

4. Non-Surfing Mexico 27

5. Valle Dorado/Puerto Vallarta – Transition Days (Days 30 to 32) 48

6. Sarteneja, Belize (Days 33 to 38) 55

7. Orange Walk & Lamanai, Belize (Days 39 to 42) 74

8. San Ignacio, Belize, Tikal and Flores, Guatemala (Days 43 to 47).... 84

9. Chiquimula, Guatemala (Days 48 to 49) 97

10. Gualan/Santiago, Guatemala (Days 50 to 52) 109

11. Livingston, Guatemala (Days 53 to 58) 120

12. Placencia, Belize (Days 59 to 62) 131

13. Caye Caulker, Belize (Days 63 to 71) 135

14. South Africa – Arrival and Zulu Nyala Safari (Days 72 to 80) 148

15. Endoneni Cheetah Project & Bayete Zulu Game Reserve, KwaZulu Natal, South Africa (Day 77) 165

16. St Lucia, KwaZulu Natal, South Africa (Days 81 to 83) 181

17. St. Lucia, Durban, Port Shepstone, East London & Addo Elephant Park (Days 84 to 88) 194

18. Storms River Mouth, Plettenberg Bay & Robberg Marine/Nature Reserve, Western Cape (Days 89 to 90) 205

19. Knysna, the Southern Tip of Africa & Hermanus, Western Cape, South Africa (Days 91 to 94) 219

20. Arrival in Cape Town & Hout Bay, Western Cape, South Africa (Days 95 to 98) 231

21. Cape Town, Western Cape, South Africa (Days 99 to 104) 243

22. Cape Town to Bulawayo, Zimbabwe (Days 105 - 107)............... 261

23. Bulawayo, Zimbabwe (Days 108 to 110).................................... 266

24. Victoria Falls, Zimbabwe (Days 111 to 112) 276

25. Chobe National Park, Botswana (Day 113) 286

26. Victoria Falls, Zimbabwe - Part II (Days 114 to 118) 295

27. Watamu, Kalifi County, Kenya – A Rocha (Days 119 to 141) 314

28. Watamu, Kenya - People.. 325

29. LUMO Community Wildlife Sanctuary, Taita Taveta District, Kenya and wrap up in Watamu (Days 142 to 153) 336

Prologue - Why I decided to write a book

It had been almost exactly a year since we returned to the "real world" when I realized that I still wasn't doing anything with the stories, the experiences and the lessons from our 14 months on the road. In many ways I was letting them all die without seeing the light of day.

Sure, my husband Daryle and I had gotten together with friends and family to share highlights, but we rarely got past favorite places, least favorite places, a chronological listing of destinations or, for the really hardy, a brief recounting of the first three months. No one ever heard about month 12 or really much past month five. Mostly we ended up telling the same few stories over and over, even if they weren't the best ones.

I kept coming back to the desire to share the overall experience. People seemed to want to hear, but the realities of busy schedules and attention spans, mine included, precluded a real sharing of the deeper essence of the trip. After dozens of cups of coffee and lunches, I'd come to the realization that we would never really be able to share our journey like that, in one sitting. We'd only ever scratch the surface. That kind of brief, superficial telling would never be fair to the experience or the audience. When I thought harder, it became obvious that realization shouldn't have come as a surprise. After all, we were gone for 14 months – that's 60 weeks; 426 days; or 10,224 hours! Why would I think we could cover it, or even sum it up, over a cup of coffee?

I also came to realize that a trip of this magnitude takes time to process, and that to a large extent, I hadn't taken the time to really examine the experience myself. I knew I'd been changed by the journey, but articulating how, that was another thing altogether. When we returned to Colorado, we jumped right back into the town and life we had left. The day after we drove back into town, I was at the store buying clothes for a job interview the next day. Within two weeks we had an apartment to paint and furnish and I had a new job doing roughly the same thing I'd been doing before. We were feeling ready to put down some semblance of roots again, and we were out of money.

I found that being immediately reabsorbed in the familiar life we'd left behind meant that reflection came slowly, in fits and starts, if at all. After a year, the stories inside began crying to be let out, not to be forgotten and left to die unheard. The process of writing this book has helped me take the time to examine the trip and its impact on me, to think about what travel has taught me and to keep those lessons alive.

By writing it all down, I intend to give you, the reader, the option to choose the stories you want to hear, from the destinations that are interesting to you, and on the time schedule that suits you. I've taken what seemed like an overwhelming amount of information, a seemingly endless collection of experiences, and fit them in to a format where they can be enjoyed in their entirety or in bits and pieces.

I'm going to do my best to write things as they really happened. I don't intend to make things up or embellish, but there are bound to be some errors, because if we've learned anything in the year we were traveling, it's the faultiness of memory! There are things Daryle and I remember completely differently, and aside from a few notes and 25,000 photos, there's no way to know which version is the real one, if in fact either really is. In all probability, it's some third option. But I promise to do my best.

Life moves pretty fast. If you don't stop and look around once in a while, you could miss it.

— Ferris Bueller

1. How we came to take our "trip of a lifetime."

In 2011, Daryle and I had been married for about ten years, always having the vague dream of "traveling more." We were planning to spend our tenth anniversary in Mexico and prior to heading out on that journey, we were doing a lot of reflecting. I was seeing 40 rapidly approaching and Daryle was already there. Milestones like 10 years of marriage or four decades of life have an uncanny way of making you acutely aware of the all too rapid passage of time.

We weren't actually getting significantly closer to that "traveling more" goal and in fact, we realized, we weren't actually clear on what we meant by "traveling more". We both knew for sure that this was no way to reach a goal.

Technically we were "traveling more," but it was clear we weren't meeting our own expectations or definition. We wanted more, much more. We'd taken a few two-week trips, we'd left the country a few times, but at this rate we knew we'd barely make a dent in our extensive travel wish lists even if we lived to be 100.

We realized that as with many things, there would be no "perfect time" and that now was very likely the best we were going to get. We recognized that we were at a point where we had to decide if we were serious about this "traveling more" thing or not. Get moving or let it go. When we took this black and white perspective, the choice became simple. Letting the dream go just wasn't an option.

"Are you more likely to regret doing this or not doing it?" Since Daryle first used this question to help me make a tough work-related decision, it had become an instrumental tool in helping me discern the right path, the path of least regret, by making the answer to tough do-or-do-not questions instantly clear. As in most cases, the answer here was decisively that we would be more likely to regret inaction.

We knew that to make "traveling more" a reality we'd need to make travel a real goal instead of just a dream. We'd need to define what our actual goal was and focus our energy. In fact, we knew we'd need to make travel THE goal. We decided that traveling more meant looking at those travel wish lists, picking a handful of items and making them happen. NOW.

What we had was a desire to travel and a willingness to take risks. What we didn't have was a lot of money, or jobs that afforded a lot of paid vacation time. There were so many places we wanted to go and we felt like we needed to make up for some lost time. We'd gone nearly 40 years with just a handful of relatively small trips and the wish lists were long – African safari, Oktoberfest in Munich, learning to surf, and just getting out of the familiar and "seeing the world."

As we looked at these tremendously long travel wish lists, we saw not just a lot of places, but a lot of faraway places. On the top of my list was an African safari. Some places are just hard to travel to for a short period of time, and Africa is one of them. We had already purchased a five-day safari at a charity auction, and we could easily have done a nice two-week vacation. However, if we were going to spend several thousand dollars on airfare and travel for 24 hours across a collection of time zones, I thought we should consider staying for more than a week or two. As I began researching, I realized that once we'd purchased the airline tickets to South Africa, it didn't actually cost that much more to stay for three months and hit Zimbabwe, Kenya and Botswana as well. On top of that, we could take time to adjust and settle in.

From experience, I now know that after making a trek like that, I want very much to sleep for about 24 hours and that it isn't until the 3rd or 4th day that I start to feel normal again. Once I threw in a few days on the other end to readjust after returning to the States, that was half of a standard American two-week vacation without seeing any elephants at all.

We knew we didn't have a lot of money to spend on a trip, but we were both at points in our lives where we were ready to make job changes. We started thinking that for us, maybe it was the right time for that long trip we'd always dreamed of. I was going to be job hunting anyway, and I figured some time off to travel wasn't really going to hurt me in the long run. Sure some might hold the gap in my employment history against me, but I figured the employers I was interested in working for would see it as an example of a go-getter setting ambitious goals and making things happen. I knew it was a risk, but it was a smaller risk than that of regretting getting this close to actually taking the trip of a lifetime and letting the opportunity slip away. I firmly believe there is nothing worse than regret and "what might have been."

At some point in our planning, we realized that making the trip longer didn't add additional negatives but would afford us more opportunity. In travel you need either time or money; in many cases they're interchangeable. Since we didn't have money, we decided we could carve out time.

Basically, we felt that if we were going to quit our jobs and sell our house, we sure as hell weren't going to do it just for a one-month vacation. If we were going all in, we were going ALL IN. We decided to aim for a year. Honestly, I think a year was an arbitrarily long time - the romanticized ideal. Like everyone who longs to travel, we'd heard of those brave souls who "take a year off" and the idea inspired us – we felt we were up for a life-disrupting challenge. Not only would we leave for a year, but we'd also sell everything and decide later on "when" and "to where" we'd return.

There was one big difference between us and most of the "year-off" stories we read; we weren't 20-somethings fresh out of college and we weren't retirees. We were firmly middle-class and middle-aged. We had a mortgage, commitments, bills and a bit of debt. We had decent jobs we mostly enjoyed, a nice, if tiny, house in a popular college town, two cars and an accumulation of decent possessions. We weren't running from anything or dealing with a life crisis. We were happy, but perhaps a bit restless. The only thing we were running from was routine. We were bored, discontent, too comfortable. I'd prefer to put it differently though, and say we were running toward something – a more informed, full and meaningful life.

At this point, we got specific and focused, and started working with what we had. We picked a departure date – April 1, 2013 - just over a year in the future. We started brainstorming about where we should go and figuring out how much money we reasonably needed to save. We started focusing every bit of energy and every cent toward making this trip happen. We opened a savings account dedicated to our trip; we stopped buying things we wouldn't need in a year when we were on the road. We started selling things we didn't use or didn't really love. We started looking for every way possible to stretch our money further.

We were in this hyper-focused life state for about 15 months from the time we decided to make the dream a reality until the day we left. This was long enough to be able to save enough money and get the necessary details in place to leave our lives for an extended period, but not so long that our departure seemed too distant or unreal. This wasn't someday, this was now and it was obvious from this point on there were plans to be made and there was no time to waste.

Throughout the planning process, I kept asking myself what I was hoping to get out of this trip. It's not that I wasn't sure about the decision. I knew without a doubt, we needed to do this. I just kept feeling like I needed to have some higher purpose than just "wanting to see the world." I struggled with the fact that I wasn't on any sort of particular quest. I wasn't looking to find myself, to recover from a particularly rough patch of life or to accomplish some ambitious task like visiting every continent. I hadn't lost my job or gone through the death of a loved one. I just wanted to see the world. I wanted to see places I hadn't seen, meet people I hadn't met and live a life where every day was not incredibly reminiscent of the day before.

I was looking for the heightened sense of being alive that comes with breaking out of routines, doing things that aren't comfortable and letting a little risk into your life. The quote I kept coming back to was one from Mary Oliver's poem The Summer Day: "Tell me, what is it you plan to do with your one wild and precious life?" It didn't seem to me I was doing all that much with my one wild and precious life.

Is it really ok for life to be fine, ok, acceptable? Shouldn't it rather be amazing, inspiring and exciting? I believe the latter and I felt like it was time to live like it. I wanted to know what it was like to live in places and ways that I'd never thought about. I wanted to enlarge my world view and my comfort zone.

And I wanted to see elephants.

2. Leaving Home

We left the U.S. on April 1, 2013, just as we had set out in our plan 15 months earlier. We weren't rigidly set on that date, but we were pretty laser-focused all year, and I don't think it's a coincidence that when it came time to buy our first tickets, April 1 turned out to be the cheapest date and the obvious choice.

It hadn't been an easy road and we were relieved to have actually made it. There was never any question, but there had certainly been challenges.

One of those challenges was money. We were planning an incredibly low-budget trip, but even so, with such a short time frame we were working toward a pretty aggressive savings goal. In addition to paying off several thousand dollars of debt, we'd been aiming to save $30,000 before leaving which would give us roughly $80/day to work with if we were gone for a year. I had planned to save up my vacation time and work right up until we left, earning a few weeks' extra travel cash. Instead, two months before our departure I found myself feeling ill.

I have a lot of faith in my immune system and it rarely lets me down so I figured it was just a particularly nasty cold or at worst maybe a bout of the flu. I made sure to get lots of sleep, but kept pushing on until one night, I lay awake alternating between convulsive shivering and profuse sweating, too weak to even think about getting out of bed. I knew a trip to the doctor could no longer be avoided.

In the morning, I felt a bit better and managed to slowly and carefully navigate the ladder steps from our loft bedroom to the main level. However, just walking across the room left me panting like I'd run a mile at top speed.

I was diagnosed with a nasty case of pneumonia and spent the next two weeks completely incapacitated. I have never been so sick that all I could possibly muster up the energy for was sleeping. The trip, work and everything else went completely on the back burner. The only thing that couldn't be put off, however, was the sale of our house. Coincidentally, our house had gone on the market the day I landed in urgent care. If you've sold a house, you know that each showing requires the house to be in pristine condition and empty, as in no one home, and that often they are scheduled with little notice. During these few weeks, we had three to four showings a day and each time, I would drag myself out of bed, we would straighten up as best we could and then we'd miserably wait it out at a coffee shop. It was a long couple of weeks – and good bye extra vacation pay.

Even closer to our scheduled departure, we made the drive to Lawrence, Kansas, where my cousin Jen lived. She and her family had agreed to give our kitty, Noir, a home while we were gone. Of all of the trip preparations, this was the single hardest thing we had to do. Our kitty was a former feral and while she was friendly and comfortable with us, she was still pretty averse to all other humans and unfamiliar with long drives in the car. She cried most of the10-hour trip. As soon as we released her in the house, she fled to the basement and hid, only venturing out at night to visit our bedroom where she repeatedly and clumsily launched herself to the five-foot window sills in a bid to escape. She was obviously terrified and it was heart-wrenching. After two days in Kansas we had to head home, with Noir still petrified and firmly wedged behind a bookshelf in the basement.

That night, instead of being back home in Colorado, we found ourselves sitting in a hotel room in the middle of Kansas, having been forced off the highway by a snowstorm, and feeling like truly awful human beings. We were the only people Noir had deemed worthy of trust in her seven years of life and we'd just abandoned her.

At this point my phone rang. It was our realtor delivering news of the first actual offer on our house. While houses around us had been selling like hotcakes, ours had been on the market for over a month and this was our first offer. At first this seemed like good news, but our excitement quickly cooled. The offer was so low we couldn't even legitimately consider it. We were counting on some money from the sale of the house to fund a portion of our trip and this offer would have left nothing, barely covering the realtor fees and mortgage payoff.

That evening in western Kansas was the only point at which I remember thinking, "Maybe this isn't such a good idea. Really, what the hell are we doing?" This was the most difficult point of the entire preparation period for both Daryle and me. We even discussed driving back to Lawrence, picking up Noir and going home. However, despite the fact that we had this conversation, we both knew deep down that going back wasn't really an option. As hard as this was, we both knew that forward was the only way to go, even if it was one difficult step at a time. That night in Kansas was definitely a difficult step, filled with sadness, tears and doubt.

Thankfully, this was a brief episode of uncertainty and once we were back in Fort Collins excitement quickly took over again. In general, things kept falling into place. By the time we left on April 1, our material possessions had been culled to the packs on our backs plus two mountain bikes and a small collection of mementos and favorite items stashed in the basement of some good-hearted friends. One car had been sold already and the other left with a trusted friend to sell once we left the country. Our house was in the final stages of being sold (at a reasonable price), with my parents entrusted with power of attorney to sign the final documents via FedEx and internet.

On March 31, we took one emotional last look around our first and only owned home, locked the door and drove away. It was odd to lock up the doors like we had so many times over the previous ten years and to walk away knowing this time we wouldn't be back. I felt unsettled and overwhelmed as we drove

16

away, but again these feelings quickly gave way to excitement about the journey we were embarking on.

We dropped a few last minute items off at our "storage unit" and my parents, who'd come to visit and help out, drove us to our airport hotel. The next morning at 5 a.m. we all took the hotel shuttle to Denver International Airport, my parents headed back home to Pennsylvania and us to Mexico to begin our adventure.

Over the next 14 months, we'd visit 23 countries and 23 U.S. states. We'd stay in hostels, hotels and on strangers' couches, travel by airplane, ferry, train, even camel, and we'd see what it was like to live on the road.

And we'd see elephants, lots and lots of elephants, starting far sooner than we expected. This book is the story of our first 6 months on the road traveling in Central America and Africa.

3. Sayulita, Mexico (Days 1 to 29)

We had decided early on in our planning that our first stop would be Sayulita, a small town about an hour north of Puerto Vallarta on the western coast of Mexico. We'd spent three days there on a previous trip and fallen in love with the quiet combination of Mexican fishing village and tourist-friendly surf town.

We'd thought, correctly it turns out, that after all the work required to "leave our lives" for a year that we'd need a chance to relax before setting off into uncharted territory. We wanted to start our trip with a low-key vacation.

Since we'd been in Sayulita before, we knew we would feel comfortable, but wouldn't be bored. We had barely scratched the surface in regard to getting acquainted with the town, its people and all it had to offer on our previous trip and there was much exploring still to be done. Sayulita also happened to have perfect waves for fledgling surfers.

We had already learned that we're not good sit-on-the-beach-and-read travelers, at least not for more than a day or two, and we'd never been on a month-long vacation. We thought we could benefit from creating some loose structure even for the "vacation" portion of our trip. The plan was for me to address the "Learn to Surf" entry on my bucket list and for Daryle to do some writing. Each morning, I'd walk the half mile to the beach from our cabin to rent a surfboard, while Daryle wrote in the courtyard. Then in the afternoon we'd meet up and go exploring.

Over the first 30 days of our trip, I did learn to surf. I also learned something much more important to life. I learned to relax.

I'd been wanting to learn to surf pretty much since I knew surfing was a thing. Even though I grew up several hours from the ocean, surrounded by farmland, where surfing was virtually unheard of, I knew instinctively that I would love it.

After my first lesson on our previous trip to Sayulita, I also knew it was going to take some work. I stood up my first time out and I was hooked. However, as amazing as it felt to pop up and ride a wave in to shore, I was pretty sure that given the titanic size of the board I was on and my complete reliance on an instructor to select the wave and give me a push with just the right timing and speed, that this didn't technically count as learning to surf. Day two of my initial surfing experience confirmed this. I took out a slightly smaller board and found that I could barely lie on my belly and paddle without falling off, never mind stand up. I proceeded to get pummeled by the surf for hours, not once getting up any farther than my knees.

My mission upon arriving in town was to decide who could provide the best lesson to get me started on my quest to actually learn to surf. Between TripAdvisor, a website for rating hotels, restaurants and things to do in locations all over the world, and some local recommendations, I settled on Lunazul Surf School. I was very pleased with my choice and not only got a few great lessons, but felt I made friends as well.

One day, less than a week in, I came in to the shop to rent a board and was unexpectedly greeted with an embrace and a kiss on each cheek by my rather handsome instructor, Viktor. Although this is a common greeting in many places, even among strangers, it wasn't common in the more reserved circles I run in and I hadn't experienced it yet on our trip. I was caught completely off-guard by the familiarity of the gesture, and although secretly thrilled, I was sure I'd been mistaken for someone else. Perhaps my expression betrayed my surprise, because although greetings were always friendly, they were never this enthusiastic again. I have to admit, I was a little disappointed.

While it seems now that I was up and catching waves in no time, that's not exactly how it felt at the time. I took an initial lesson that refreshed what I had learned the previous year and that got me relatively proficient at getting to my feet, or so I thought. I had a few good days, and then I had days that were frustrating and discouraging, when it didn't seem like I was improving. I'd have a decent day and then a mediocre day and then a day where I just got beat up by the ocean for a few hours. Some days it seemed like I wasn't going to learn to surf after all.

The weird thing is that within a few weeks, looking back, I could hardly remember those feelings of frustration and doubt. I have journal pages filled with them, so I know they were real, but once I did start catching my own waves, those feelings were very quickly forgotten – replaced with determination, confidence and pure joy. It's easy to forget how much work something took to learn, once you catch on.

I took a second lesson a little over a week in, which was a turning point. In this lesson, Viktor, taught me some key things and the next day, I caught several of my very own waves! I don't think it's a stretch to say that the essential lessons I learned for surfing are also basic lessons for travel, and even life in general, so I'd like to share them here.

1. Chill out – I learned to relax and just enjoy myself. In April, the good waves were sometimes few and far between, but I was sitting in the ocean on a beautiful sunny day with more of the same stretching out in front of me. There was no reason not to relax and enjoy it. Even if the perfect waves weren't showing up at the moment, I was in a pretty sweet spot. Probably relaxing is

something I should inherently know how to do, but I've found I need to be reminded over and over – and I don't think I'm alone.

2. Recognize the right opportunity – In order to not miss the best waves, I needed to know what a good wave looked like and then be patient. I couldn't go after every wave that rolled in. I'd seen plenty of times that if I got frustrated and took a mediocre wave because I was tired of waiting, without fail, I would see a perfect wave coming in while I was paddling back out to the lineup. I learned that it was important to be confident that I could identify a good wave and then to wait. The more time I spent in the water, the more confident I became.

3. Identify the right spot to be and stay there – In my second lesson, Viktor had taught me how to figure out where I needed to be to catch the waves, to set markers on the horizon that would help me recognize my spot, and then stick to it. I might get distracted talking to a friend or watching some fish, the current might gradually pull me away from my spot, but I had to keep checking my markers and make sure I got myself back to that right spot or I'd never catch anything.

4. Go for it! When I saw a good wave coming and I was in the right spot, it was like magic. I'd turn around and paddle like crazy with all the energy I had…and I'd catch that wave. I'd find myself flying over the water with addictive speed and control – at least for a few seconds. Those seconds were totally worth all the effort and waiting.

Like many things surfing is simple; not to be confused with easy – two completely different things. I learned that surfing, like life, is about being where you need to be, recognizing the right opportunities and working like hell to grab hold of them…and in between, chilling out and enjoying the moment.

4. Non-Surfing Mexico

Whether you come to Sayulita to surf or not, you can't miss that surfing has made the town what it is. There are countless surf schools lining the downtown streets, kiosks renting boards littering the beach and the water at the main beach is constantly filled with beginners, like me, from 9-to-5. In the evening, on days when the surf is especially good, the beginners clear out and you can watch the pros catch the waves.

I didn't spend all my time in Sayulita surfing, really just a few hours a day, and unfortunately only for the first two weeks. About two weeks in I started to experience pretty severe pain in a few of my ribs, enough that walking hurt and sleeping on my left side was impossible. I attempted to keep surfing (did I mention that I am stubborn?), until a final fall made it impossible to get back on my board and incredibly difficult to even get back to shore, bobbing along pathetically using the board for support and flotation. At that point I gave in and started Googling broken ribs. There's no hospital in Sayulita, and my research turned up basically no treatment for either bruised or broken ribs beyond rest, so I decided no doctor was necessary and I'd just take it easy. The most severe pain subsided within a few weeks, and after several months I was good as new (which is good because by then, we were in Africa).

Over the course of our month in Sayulita, we gradually got accustomed to making things up as we went along. We learned to form a general idea for the day, rather than make a specific schedule, to savor the moment a bit more and to revel in the unusual. Our sense of adventure started to unfurl.

Learning to relax was the first step in this transition. At first, not having a daily routine or a set of things I was "supposed" to do was incredibly uncomfortable. I am a fairly driven person, relying heavily on my goals and to-do lists to structure my days. Every day it got easier though, and I adjusted much more quickly than I anticipated.

About two weeks into our time in Sayulita, Daryle had scheduled an interview with a local artist, and although nothing was mentioned at the meeting, he told me later that evening that there had been a subtle feeling of something being off, possibly of unspoken expectations not being met.

At this point we began comparing notes from our first two weeks in Mexico and piecing together clues. For example, our first morning in Sayulita, I had gone to the surf shop at 8 a.m. to rent a board. They were still hauling the boards out and getting ready for the day. I had to wait a bit before they were ready to actually let me take a board. Yet a few days later, I was showing up just after 8 a.m. and things were all set out and seemed to have been ready to go for some time. Curious, but I never thought too much about it.

With these bits of anecdotal evidence, we started to wonder if our clock was off. We knew that despite their proximity, there was a weird time zone relationship between Puerto Vallarta (where our plane landed) and Sayulita. They are in different states and technically different time zones. However, to prevent tourists in Sayulita from missing their planes in Puerto Vallarta, Sayulita pretty much operates on Puerto Vallarta time. We were familiar with this complication from our previous trip though, and we were positive we had the right time when we arrived, so how could things have gone wrong?

With a little internet research, we quickly learned that Mexico, like much of the U.S., practices daylight-saving time. The spring forward, however, happens in April rather than March, like in the States. Since we'd already "sprung forward" in March before leaving Colorado, it never occurred to us we'd need to do it again in Sayulita.

This oversight was made possible by two factors – we didn't have many places to be, and the people in Sayulita were apparently never going to fault us for being late (at least they weren't going to mention it).

The next morning, I walked bashfully into the surf shop and profusely apologized to Viktor. I had been a full hour late to my lesson the week prior. He had never mentioned it, the day of the lesson or on any of my subsequent daily visits to rent a board. Although, when I finally broached the subject, he broke into a wide grin and started to laugh.

The fact that it took almost two weeks to realize our oversight inadvertently confirmed that our transition to winging it and operating on a more relaxed schedule was going well.

In addition to relaxing, we soaked in the simplicity of living in a studio cabin with what we could fit in two carry-on bags and two small daypacks. We walked everywhere and savored every unrushed minute. We ate dirt-cheap fresh veggies and fruit bought from dozens of small produce shops, enjoyed all kinds of street tacos, some particularly delicious pizza made by an Italian expat, and fresh baked goods sold by a couple out of the back of their station wagon.

We would intentionally wander the town square area in the evenings on the lookout for that pastry car. We couldn't discern any particular schedule, so we never knew when they would show up, but we didn't want to miss it when they did.

We learned to cultivate our sense of adventure and to embrace the unexpected. One morning on our way to breakfast we were walking along the dirt road running through our neighborhood when we turned a corner and ran smack dab into an elephant. Yep, an elephant, in Mexico. I was very surprised and quite thrilled. I hadn't expected to see my first elephant for months.

Later that day, we stumbled onto a huge red and yellow tent and realized the circus was in town. Over the next several days we observed that it is apparently common practice in Mexico to take one's elephant on a morning stroll through the neighborhood or to stake him out to graze along the banks of the dry riverbed running through town.

We saw the elephant in our neighborhood daily over the next week. Once ambling along the roadside, next browsing the trees along the riverbank. Always he was accompanied by an older Mexican gentleman who followed along toting a white plastic chair, for resting during more extended snacking sessions.

Some out-of-the-ordinary adventures were exciting, like the elephant, and some fascinating, like a trail of leafcutter ants we discovered outside our front door and watched over several days as they consumed an entire stem of bananas. And some were less welcome, but adventures just the same.

One morning, I was preparing to pull a dress out of my neatly folded pile of clothes. I had barely lifted a corner when I glimpsed something that definitely did not belong. You know the feeling you get when you're not sure what you just saw/heard/felt, but you know something about it was not right? I dropped the corner of fabric like a red hot coal. Although I couldn't possibly have identified anything in that split second, somewhere deep down I instinctually recognized what I'd glimpsed and "Scorpion!" is what I yelled. I immediately called Daryle over to do a closer inspection, revealing a 3-inch-long translucent yellowish critter hunkered down in the folds of my dress – a scorpion indeed.

This experience caused a bit of disillusionment with our living arrangement as well as with the perceived "deal" I believed we'd made with these arachnids. We had received instructions along with our lease agreement not to leave things on the floor of our cabin because of the possibility of scorpions hiding out in the dark crevices. I'd been dutifully storing all my items either on hooks or folded on the plentiful shelves in the bedroom.

Because of the instructions we'd been given, I had been under the impression that scorpions can't climb. Not true in fact. Some scorpions - the large scary-looking black, but not very potent scorpions - don't climb. The smaller, clearish, more potent and distinctly creepier kind though, they can climb. I generally love animals but found the warm fuzzy feeling associated with kittens and sea otters did not extend to our new arachnid friend. I refused to share my cabin with a scorpion and Daryle assisted in its permanent removal.

In an attempt to make me feel better, a friend from Hawaii, presumably with scorpion experience, shared her knowledge via Facebook that evening that scorpions are rather territorial, so once we did away with our unwanted houseguest, she thought there were unlikely to be more for a while, you know, until word got out there was a vacancy. Although I found no conclusive evidence to support this theory in a quick Google search, sometimes, I decided, you just have to believe what gets you through the night.

This began the daily ritual that would last until our arrival in Europe five months later in which I shook out my clothes before getting dressed each morning and pulled back and inspected the bed sheets before climbing in each night.

It was nearing time to leave Sayulita, but because we had made a point of keeping an eye out for opportunities to experience new things, I knew I couldn't leave without taking a cruise to Las Islas Marietas, one of the few places outside the Galapagos Islands where you can see a colony of blue-footed boobies. Since I wasn't sure when we might have the opportunity to get to the Galapagos, I thought I should probably take my chance to see these unique birds now.

I'm not usually a huge bird person and I wasn't familiar with this species ahead of time, but I was won over by their rarity, and of course their amusing name. Given their name, I thought maybe their feet would have a hint of blue, but I wasn't prepared to see birds that looked like they had stepped in a puddle of sky blue latex. Those feet are stunning and I loved these birds immediately. The blue color, I learned, is maintained by pigments in the fish they eat, and the vibrancy is indicative of immune function and health, so the bluer the feet, the more likely a bird is to find a high-quality mate. It's a fascinating way to get a date.

On the hour-long trip to see the boobies, I also saw humpback whales up close and visited a "secret" beach accessible only by swimming beneath a stone archway into a circular, open-air chamber of sorts. I also made some new friends.

Daryle wasn't particularly enamored with seeing the birds, no matter how rare, and is no huge fan of being out on the ocean, so I went this one alone. I shared the boat to Las Islas with a group of American women on a milestone birthday celebration. They were fascinated with the trip that Daryle and I were embarking on and quickly adopted me into their group.

This was an introduction to how easy it can be to meet people and make friends on the road. I found that not being in a routine made it easier for me to pay attention and to be curious and open to who and whatever came my way. Being relaxed made it easier to be friendly and strike up a casual conversation, and on the road you never know where that will lead. After spending the day together, my new friends invited Daryle and me to join them for a paella party the next evening at their rental house. They knew a guy who had started a business in Sayulita as a paella personal chef of sorts. The next night we walked over to their house where the paella chef showed up with his wife and kids, a huge paella pan and all kinds of shrimp, fish and veggies to make the biggest and most colorful pan of food I think I've ever had the privilege of witnessing or sharing.

The meal was delicious and the company enjoyable. We quickly felt included and at home with these virtual strangers.

A few days later, on a walk through town we noticed that a large banner had appeared showing a woman on horseback wearing traditional Mexican dress and advertising something called the Primer Circuito de Escaramuzas at Lienzo Charro de Sayulita.

It was scheduled for the following Sunday afternoon. We were intrigued and set about trying to figure out what an escaramuza was and where we might find Lienzo Charro de Sayulita. What was a Lienzo Charro anyway?

On the day of the advertised event, we took what turned out to be a rather long walk. We'd gotten a general idea of which direction to head and, with several stops to ask for directions, we did end up at the lienzo charro along with a few tourists and a lot of Mexicans. We had the privilege of enjoying escaramuza, an event that is often part of a larger Mexican Charreada or Charrería, similar to an American rodeo, and the national sport of Mexico. A lienzo charro, it turns out, is basically a rodeo arena, and most towns have one.

Directly translated, escaramuza means "skirmish" and has historical roots in the Mexican revolution. An escaramuza team, is made up of eight young women wearing beautiful, bright-colored, full-skirted folk dresses, and their well-trained horses. Together, they ride intricately choreographed routines that include quick turns, pirouettes and often horses crossing paths in the center of the arena at high speed.

It is a competition, and teams are scored according to the precision and difficulty of their routines. The event we saw was among teams from six neighboring cities, including Sayulita. Unfortunately, I can't really tell you who won. I'm still not sure. But I can tell you we had a great time experiencing a part of Mexican culture previously unknown to us. And I had my first elote (technically elote en vaso, simply corn in a cup), a common street food combining warm corn off the cob, sour cream, cheese, sometimes mayonnaise, chile, lime juice and salt served in a Styrofoam cup. Delicioso!

As we began to see our month in Sayulita coming to a close, we knew we wouldn't experience the luxury of this kind of stability for a while, so we also took the time to nail down the schedule and details for Phase 2 of the trip – five weeks in Belize and Guatemala.

We had long been proponents of Couchsurfing.org, a website that connects travelers with hosts who have a free bed or couch. The deal is that there is no exchange of money; that's what makes it different from Airbnb, VRBO or any number of other short-term rental websites. We run into people all the time who cannot fathom staying with a stranger, but we've had incredibly positive experiences. However, we do our due diligence and only stay with people who have been positively reviewed and with whom we seem to have at least a few things in common.

We lined up a Couchsurfing host in Puerto Vallarta for two nights and a flight to Chetumal on the Caribbean coast. We finalized plans with members of two Rotary Clubs in Guatemala that had offered to host us through a connection to my Club back home, and we made reservations for our first few nights in Belize. We generally tried to book accommodations at least a day or two in advance and to avoid showing up in a new town without a reservation for at least one night, but we also rarely booked more than a two-night stay (in case we hated the place or saw somewhere else we absolutely needed to stay). We were always trying to balance spontaneity with the risk of winding up sleeping on a park bench.

Relaxed and with our appetites whetted for new experiences and our eyes peeled for exotic adventures, we felt ready to head off into slightly more uncharted territory. But first, a brief two-day intermission in the tourist city of Puerto Vallarta.

5. Valle Dorado/Puerto Vallarta – Transition Days (Days 30 to 32)

Sayulita is a great place to hang out and relax, but if you need to buy toothpaste or malaria medicine, Puerto Vallarta is a much better bet. We knew that once we hit Belize, the availability of goods would plummet, so we took advantage of our time in Puerto Vallarta to restock at Wal-Mart and Chendrai (the Mexican grocery superstore).

We had contacted and been accepted by our first Couchsurfing host of the trip, Alma, a bilingual young Mexican woman who lived with her Spanish-speaking mother and daughter in a sparse apartment just north of Puerto Vallarta, in the suburb of Valle Dorado.

We caught a bus south and then took a taxi to her home. Once Alma walked us to the nearest bus stop from her apartment though, we were able to manage by bus for the next few days.

While transportation was straightforward, communication proved more difficult. Alma was away at work for the majority of the day and her daughter at school, leaving us at home with her mother who spoke no English. This was the first real test of my Spanish skills. Sayulita had been enough of a tourist town that most people we'd encountered spoke better English than I spoke Spanish, and I'd been able to be lazy.

I could get by in communication about basic facts and pleasantries, like "hello, nice to meet you" and "can you tell me where the bus stop is?", but it didn't take long to realize I was still far from able to have a meaningful conversation. Alma's mother and I got along fine but a bit awkwardly, with me carefully and painstakingly rehearsing each sentence in my head before speaking, and then failing to comprehend the reply until the third or fourth attempt. I really wanted to get to know her and was frustrated that I just didn't have the skills, or ultimately the patience, to get beyond the basic necessities. There are few things I find as frustrating as listening to someone talk and realizing I have no idea what they're trying to tell me despite how hard I am trying. Asking someone to repeat something a fifth time is my personal hell.

The next day, after breakfast, Alma headed off to work and we took the bus into Puerto Vallarta. We still had some plans to finalize for the next leg of our trip and needed to check email and since Alma didn't have an internet connection at her home, we went in search of one elsewhere.

We've discovered that if you dress well when traveling it can go a long way in getting you leeway with rules. Pair that with being friendly and acting like you belong, and you can get away with a lot. We picked out a nice hotel with a comfortable-looking lobby, discretely used our phones to verify the presence of an open Wi-Fi network and then settled in on a couch like we were hotel guests, as we pulled out our laptops and got to work responding to emails and updating our blogs. Once we had the online items checked off our list, we moved on to the errands we hoped to accomplish.

I had chosen to buy malaria pills in the U.S. because I had good insurance and a doctor who had been willing to write me a prescription for a 90-day supply, and also because I don't like to wing it with things like potentially life-saving medication. Daryle on the other hand did not have great insurance and is more willing to make things up as he goes. He had also succeeded in getting a 90-day prescription before we left Colorado, but when the pharmacy called to see if we were sure we wanted them to fill the prescription because it was "very expensive," we balked at the $1,000 price tag. Even I agreed there had to be a better way. So it was that we found ourselves in Puerto Vallarta looking up local pharmacies on Google. The cheapest option for malaria-prevention that would be effective against the mosquitos we'd encounter in both Central America and Africa was doxycycline hyclate, a pill taken daily starting a day or two before potential exposure and continuing almost a month after leaving an infected area.

Armed with the appropriate drug name on a slip of paper, we went from pharmacy to pharmacy, finally succeeding in finding a 50-day supply. for 150 pesos. That's about $9US - less than the cost of one pill in the States. Combined with what I was already carrying, that would be enough to get us through our time in Africa. We had to go to several pharmacies to secure the full 50-day supply, but for over 98% cost savings that seemed more than reasonable. No prescription, no hassle – one pharmacist even called around to find out which location had the largest supply for us before we traipsed all over town.

Beyond that, errands were easy and relatively familiar. Wal-Mart is pretty much the same anywhere and we had no trouble picking up a few forgotten toiletries. We then headed on to Chendrai – unknowingly beginning what would become one of our favorite travel habits over the course of our trip – visiting local grocery stores. Whether a small roadside stand or a supermarket, perusing the aisles of food became one of our favorite ways to get to know a new place. We were able to eat inexpensively while still trying all the local delicacies, and also to learn what ingredients figured prominently in local cuisine.

Chendrai was much like our huge stores back home with a plethora of options and many of the same products. However, a few things caught our eye, like an entire aisle of instant coffee, and a swimming pool size bin of limes. A few items we were less familiar with were also on display, such as Jamaica (hibiscus) flowers, tamarind pods, and an octopus simply draped over a huge ice block in the seafood section.

We passed on the octopus and instead picked up a few packs of what we'd come to refer to affectionately as "mexicookies" for the plane ride. Mexicookies are any of the hundreds of varieties of inexpensive packaged cookies sold pretty much anywhere food is sold in Mexico – bus stations, thatch-roofed kiosks or supermarkets. They became a staple snack, with the Emperador lime sandwich cookie topping my favorite list.

Relaxed and with everything once again in order, we were ready to move on to Belize. We packed up our bags, enjoyed a final breakfast with our hosts and caught a bus to the airport. Amazingly of the 23 flight segments over the course of our entire trip, the next two were the only ones that experienced delays. We were 40 minutes late into Mexico City (no big deal, we still caught our connection), and then just miles from our final destination of Chetumal, we were diverted 190 miles north to Merida. I was concerned we would be stranded in Merida at midnight with no reservations, but we actually just refueled and continued immediately on to Chetumal. The bad weather was apparently short-lived. Since we'd been living in a pretty rustic cabin for the past month, we were looking forward to the comforts of a modern chain hotel. We'd had blown a whole day's budget ($86) booking a Holiday Inn and had our hopes up.

We arrived a bit after midnight looking forward to our comfy bed. As we opened the door, I let out that arriving-home-after-a-long-day sigh of relief. A split second later, I noticed the huge puddle of what I hoped was water, in the middle of the tile floor. I was tired and as I stood there I felt tears welling up – the I-know-this-is-not-a-big-deal-but-I'm-exhausted kind of tears. We had an early morning appointment with a bus and all I wanted to do was crawl into bed and sleep. It was a tough decision between trekking back to the front desk to ask for another room and just carefully walking around the puddle and collapsing into bed. We stood there with our packs still on, staring at the puddle and then the bed, and then back to the puddle again. I'd like to say we walked around the puddle and just fell into bed – it would make a better story and show what seasoned, no-nonsense travelers we were – but that's not what happened.

Ever the practical one, I realized how much grumpier I would be at 3 a.m. when I walked through the offending puddle on the way to the bathroom. I sighed heavily as we turned to trudge down the three flights of stairs back to the lobby. In hindsight, I realize I had no idea what exhausted really looked like yet. In another month or two, I wouldn't have batted an eyelash at a trivial puddle and would have been asleep in that bed already.

6. Sarteneja, Belize (Days 33 to 38)

The next morning, we were up at dawn to catch a bus to Belize. For us, Belize was a measured step into the unknown. We'd been to Belize, ridden the public buses and explored the coast and jungle for 10 days in 2011. On our current trip, we intended to revisit a few favorite places, but mostly to see the parts of the country we'd missed on our first trip. We hadn't even set foot in the entire southern half of the country.

One of the first things we'd noticed on our first trip that sets Belize apart from its neighbors is a complete lack of corporate chain businesses. You will not find a Wal-Mart, and you won't see a McDonald's or a KFC, not even in the country's largest city. As Central American countries go, Belize is expensive and hard to navigate by public transportation because so much is located away from the main highways.

Belize has very few roads that aren't dirt, just three main paved two-lane "highways" – one north to south, one east to west and one shorter diagonal connector in the middle that cuts directly to the capital of Belmopan from the southern coast. Getting into the jungle or countryside really requires a car, and getting to the hundreds of small islands off the coast, called cayes (pronounced keys, like what you use to unlock your front door) requires a water taxi or charter. Once you've seen the roads in Belize you begin to understand why all rentals seem to be four-wheel drive and rates are higher than in the U.S. On our first trip, we'd rented a car from a gas station that came with instructions not to drive through the river, which we quickly found to be an unreasonable request. We'd also found ourselves navigating a road that had gradually gotten so steep and narrow that there was no way to turn around. She had sucked us in with her mystery of what was around the next bend until we were stuck.

As the road got steeper and steeper, narrower and narrower, we just hoped it wouldn't dead end. As we rounded the sixth or seventh 270-degree curve, we finally glimpsed the bottom, a straight section of road running along a river. This is where we ran into the rather grouchy owner of the private driveway we'd inadvertently just navigated. Apparently it had cost him many thousands of dollars to put in and thankfully he didn't want us mucking it up further by retracing our steps. We'd decided on our second visit that we wouldn't be renting any cars.

We decided to start this trip in the small fishing village of Sarteneja, located at the end of a 45-mile dirt road on a spit of land looking back toward the rest of Belize over the Corozal Bay. From Chetumal, this required a taxi ride to the bus terminal followed by a two-hour bus ride across the Belizean border to the town of Orange Walk and another two-and-a-half-hour bus ride over bumpy dirt roads to Sarteneja.

Unlike the long haul buses in Mexico that boast decently comfortable seats, air conditioning and frequently, an on-board bathroom, Belizean buses are retired Bluebird school buses. No air conditioning, no bathroom and very little room for luggage. Daryle and I frequently found ourselves sharing a seat, with our luggage piled in our laps and our knees jammed into the seat in front of us. Every time we unfolded ourselves from a trip like this, we were painfully reminded that school buses are crafted for a very specific audience – people much smaller and shorter than us, not to mention younger. Belizean buses are, however, quite cheap. I suppose you get what you pay for.

We'd learned an important lesson in bus selection on our first trip as well. In Belize (and many Central American countries), some routes have both "express" buses and "regular" buses. We now knew that if time was a consideration at all, we needed to make sure we got an express bus. In Belize particularly, people have not adopted the idea of bus stops per se. We'd been on a "regular" bus before and found that the driver would stop wherever there was a person waiting, even if it was 40 feet from the last person the bus had picked up. This resulted in what felt like eternal rounds of the children's playground game Red Light Green Light, where the children run while the teacher's back is turned but must come to an immediate halt as soon as she turns around again. Even though I wasn't on a set schedule, I still found this method of operation to be an unfathomable and maddening waste of time, not to mention an uncomfortable disjointed and jerky ride.

This was an early lesson for me in how mindsets are acquired, not automatic, and a product of the prevalent culture and expectations. Time efficiency doesn't seem to be a consideration in many places we visited, and Belize tops that list. If you can relax and embrace it, it's actually quite refreshing after the rushed, stressed state of the average American, but it's a marked adjustment. In my daily life, I pride myself on efficiency and productivity and while I'm willing to embrace a slower pace when traveling, I still always look for the "express" bus.

A notable exception to this laissez-faire attitude and to well, everything in Belize, is the Mennonite community – a sort of model of efficiency in the midst of a lackadaisical status quo. There is a large population of Mennonites who emigrated to Belize from Mexico (who'd emigrated from Canada before that and the Russian Empire before that). Having grown up in Lancaster County, Pennsylvania, an area with a high concentration of both Amish and Mennonite peoples, I found this particularly interesting. I am used to seeing the traditional Mennonite dress, horse and buggies, etc., but seeing those things, juxtaposed with palm trees, tropical flowers and the Latin American and Caribbean culture was incredibly bizarre.

Belizeans are typically dark-skinned. Mennonites, tending to be of German or eastern European heritage, are incredibly fair-skinned. The dress in Belize is not particularly conservative. Tight tops and short skirts are not uncommon. Mennonite men and women (and even children) on the other hand usually wear long pants or conservative dresses. Women cover their heads with bonnets or other head coverings.

Socially, Mennonites tend to be reserved and are known collectively for incredible discipline, orderliness and work ethic. When you enter a Mennonite community in Belize you feel like you've been transported to an entirely different country, not just because the people look and carry on differently, but because there are significant differences in the physical structure of the towns, the jobs people do and the products that are available. For example – when we'd visited the Mennonite community of Spanish Lookout on our trip in 2011, this was the only time in our two trips to Belize that we experienced a well-paved road with an actual painted line separating the traffic traveling in opposite directions. Suddenly, as we entered town, not just a line, but a double yellow line appeared out of nowhere. Serious farming is also much more common in the Mennonite communities of Belize. There is a dairy in Spanish Lookout with remarkable ice cream, something that is hard to find not just in Belize, but in Central America in general in our experience. This is one of the only places in this region where we saw dairy cows.

Back to the trip at hand, we were headed into Orange Walk on our "express" bus and we knew we'd have to find our next bus quickly. There was only one bus a day to Sarteneja and we didn't want to miss it. As par for the course in Belize, the bus we needed to catch departed, not from the bus terminal where our bus would drop us off but from a hotel several blocks away. We had let our bus driver know where we were headed when we boarded and had asked for directions to our bus. As we were getting off the bus, he said a few words to a Mennonite fellow who'd also been on the bus and then told us to follow him. We were still struggling into our packs as he took off down the street at a brisk clip. He wasn't running away, just not waiting around. Not wanting to lose our only guide, we took off at a slow run while hefting our packs over one shoulder and looking every bit the discombobulated tourists. We eventually caught up, and without a word, he led us zigzagging through the streets of Orange Walk, dropping us off at a bus parked alongside the road. We thanked him, he paused for just a moment, gave a friendly nod and, still without a word, continued on his way.

About an hour into this second bus ride, in the middle of sugar cane fields and not much else, we came to an unexpected stop in the middle of the road. There was truly nothing around, no intersections for miles, no other vehicles and no obvious reason to stop. My Spanish may not be amazing, but we quickly picked up that a number of passengers were giving the driver a good-natured and well-deserved ribbing for running out of gas.

About 45 minutes later, we looked out the windows to see a pickup truck full of gas cans and Belizean men pull up. Several of the guys jumped out and immediately started siphoning gas from the cans into the bus, giving the distinct impression that this was not the first time their services had been required.

With the gas tank refilled, we were able to continue on and finally arrived in Sarteneja in the late afternoon. We were anxious to stretch our legs after so much bus time, so we dropped our bags at our hostel cabin and immediately walked the mile into town to explore. From the moment we arrived and started walking around town, I was smitten.

Because of its position on the east side of the Chetumal Bay, Sarteneja is the only place in Belize where you can watch the sun set over the ocean, and our first evening in town we were rewarded with one of the most amazing sunsets I've ever seen. We sat on the pier, our feet dangling in the turquoise water, a cold Fanta in hand watching as the sun set and picturesque fishing boats bobbed slowly in the undulating sea. It was impossible not to feel completely at peace.

We didn't see many people during our time in Sarteneja, but the people we did encounter were incredibly friendly, travelers and locals alike. The local economy is based largely on lobster and conch fishing, with a growing tourism component. However, most of the travelers we met, were on longer journeys, not week-long vacations. Sarteneja doesn't make it onto the itinerary for most shorter trips for good reason. There's no airport, and the bus ride was no picnic. This is definitely a backpack-traveler kind of town.

While in Sarteneja, we stayed at a well-run, inexpensive hostel where our room consisted of a double bed and about one foot of space on each side in a little thatched hut in the woods. The bathhouse, emblazoned with a greater than life-size likeness of Bob Marley, was a short walk down the path. I found only one creepy scorpion in the shower with me all week and he was very tiny. The hostel was comfortable and cozy, and at $14US a night, it may well have been the cheapest place two people could stay in the entire country. On top of that, one of the owners ran a restaurant on-site and was a fantastic chef.

Usually, we were told, the water is crystal clear turquoise, but due to a cold front that came in just as we arrived, the water was churned up and milky. From information gleaned since our travels, the cloudiness of the water is probably a pretty standard feature due to the high density of water-soluble limestone in the area.

While in Sarteneja, every day had a new adventure, and for a
sleepy town of 4,500, we kept surprisingly busy for five days. If
travel is about new experiences – and I believe it is – then
Sarteneja was a great place to start.

One of my many goals on our trip had been to see a manatee.
I've always found them to be endearingly homely creatures and
as peaceful minders-of-their-own-business, I feel especially sad
to know they are so often injured by reckless humans. When I
noticed during the planning phase of our trip that the village of
Sarteneja was home to a manatee rehabilitation center, I briefly
got really excited. Then I noticed that it was not open to the

public, only by special appointment, and I got disappointed and wrote it off, hoping there'd be other places I could manage to see a manatee. I had forgotten all about it by the time we arrived in town.

However, almost as soon as we met the owners of our hostel, they told us there was an appointment made at the center for the following afternoon and we were welcome to come along. I immediately got very excited all over again! You'll probably quickly begin to notice that animal encounters are a recurring theme in my narrative. As a lifelong animal lover and university biology major, seeing new and different animals is one of the highlights of any trip for me.

What I saw and learned about the Manatee and Primate Rehabilitation Centre, hosted and managed by a non-profit organization called Wildtracks, was fascinating and I have seriously thought about returning as a long-term volunteer. They have an amazing and affordable volunteer program that lets the Centre accomplish a lot more than would be possible with only paid staff, while allowing volunteers the opportunity to get experience working hands on with these unique animals.

While we were at the Centre, we got to see a growing Antillean manatee named Duke who weighed in at about 200 pounds at the time of our visit. In order to start the process of being released back into the wild he'd need to be closer to 350 pounds. He had been having trouble gaining weight and was being tube-fed, a process which saves a lot of manatees but involves very specialized training. There are only about 100 people in the world who have that training we were told, and three of them reside at the Rehabilitation Centre in Sarteneja. We were able to watch as the crew weighed and fed Duke, a tedious process that necessitated the participation of a team of people and a huge sling to haul Duke up out of the pool before the feeding could even begin. Over the next hour we watched as Duke was intubated and gently pumped full of a nutritious, high-calorie liquid. It was a slow and cautious process that required not only rare expertise, but incredible patience and care.

Our tour guide, Emma, also happened to be the primary handler of a 2-month-old Yucatan black howler monkey named Bean. When Bean got a bit older, she would have far less contact with humans, but at the time of our visit, she was still very young and we were lucky enough to have her accompany us on our tour. Bean was discovered by a hiker on a trail in the Cockscomb Basin Wildlife Sanctuary in southern Belize covered by ants and in rough shape. For some reason, she'd wound up alone and on her own at only 1 week old. Luckily, someone knew to call Wildtracks and a team was sent to rescue her. When she arrived at the Centre she weighed just over 8 ounces –.that's about the weight of a hamster, or two sticks of butter if you're more familiar with kitchen measures. Now, with the help of Emma and her fellow volunteers, Bean was growing into a healthy little monkey and working toward returning to the jungle.

*At the time of writing this manuscript, a little over two years after our visit, Bean and her group, consisting of three similarly aged howlers and one spider monkey, were living in a pre-release cage in the Belize jungle where they were learning survival skills like climbing, foraging and working together as a troop. They were being weaned off human attention and were learning to focus on interacting primarily with each other. Sometime soon they were scheduled to be released fully into the wild.

On day three in Sarteneja, we borrowed a few bikes from our hostel so we could explore a bit farther afield. We'd received loose directions to several interesting sites nearby, the first of which were some Mayan ruins. Unlike all the Mayan sites we'd visited previously, these were completely unexcavated. Not knowing exactly what that would mean, we were intrigued. We followed the directions, consisting largely of statements like "turn left at the big tree" and eventually managed to find the narrow unmarked trail into the forest. At first, we weren't sure if we were in the right place, but then we started to notice a few sizeable mounds of earth covered with vegetation. On second glance, we realized how out-of-place these mounds were in the otherwise pancake-flat landscape. If we'd just stumbled upon this place, we would never have suspected we were looking at the remnants of a thousand-year-old civilization. These ruins looked deceptively unremarkable and the contrast to excavated sites we'd visited made us appreciate all the work that must have gone into unearthing the impressive structures at sites like Coba, Caracol and Tikal.

With the relatively small number of visitors to Sarteneja, sites like this one aren't well-marked or well worn, which is much of their appeal. This made me think of the huge number of historic and culturally significant sites that must exist across Central America, some perhaps not even discovered and many not developed for tourism. In fact, the challenge of preserving sites like this came to light just weeks later, when a story surfaced in the international news about a construction company in Belize that had been bulldozing a Mayan temple nearby for fill to use in road construction.

This site was well-known, located just 6 miles from the large town of Orange Walk and had over 80 buildings spread over 12 square miles. The incident caused much public outrage and resulted in fines, but it made me wonder how many lesser known and smaller sites have met similar fates with no press at all.

A theme that would recur time and time again during our travels started to take shape. What is common locally, even though rare on a worldwide scale, is chronically undervalued. Something exotic to visitors runs the risk of seeming mundane to those who experience it on a daily basis and so the things that people are willing to travel thousands of miles to see are often also the most endangered.

The next day, we again took the bikes and headed off in search of a forested cenote, following yet another set of vague directions. A cenote is a place where groundwater is accessible at the surface, often occurring when the limestone roof of a cave collapses, leaving a previously underground lake exposed. We'd encountered cenotes before and as a lover of caves and all things cave-like, I found them all fascinating. While many are in caverns and require climbing to access, this one was at ground level and uniquely surrounded by thick mangrove forest.

After trying several paths, we suddenly found ourselves standing on the edge of the 100m wide lake. With no water flowing in or out and no breeze, the surface was completely calm and we could see dozens of tiny fish flitting about in the leaf litter in the shallows.

The mangroves were so dense that getting around was possible only by weaving through tunnel-like passageways formed by mangrove trunks and roots lending the area a magical, fairytale-like quality. The frequent spider webs though – not quite so idyllic.

Once we'd explored to our hearts content, we hopped on our bikes to head home. We passed by a local woman gathering some odd-looking berries from a tree along the road. Always interested in trying new food, particularly food we might be able to pick for free, we stopped to find out what she was harvesting. She told us these were genipes, offering us a handful and explaining how to eat them.

These little fruits go by a plethora of alternative names – Spanish lime, guinep, genipe, ginepa, quenepa, quenepe, chenet, canepa, mamon, limoncillo, skinip or mamoncillo. The size of a large grape, they have a skin like a lime (but a bit thinner) that you peel off, and a large seed that you spit out after sucking off the sweet flesh of the fruit. These fruits were an especially welcome taste bud treat, as one of the shortcomings of Sarteneja had been a surprising lack of availability of fruits and vegetables – like almost none. People must rely on what grows in their yards, because they certainly don't rely on the grocery store.

Speaking of fruit, there was actually an abundance of oranges and mangoes falling from the trees back at the hostel, but none were particularly ripe, despite the fact that they fell with every breeze. The mangoes may not have been good for eating, but they were good for amusement, slamming into the metal roofs of the compound like little detonating bombs. After almost a week, you'd think I would have gotten used to the sudden noises, but I'd jump about a foot every time, much to Daryle's amusement.

Overall, we had found Sarteneja a refreshing place for a little retreat. It was incredibly peaceful because in addition to beautiful scenery and the lapping of the ocean, there was very little going on, which was great, for a time. By the time we were wrapping up day five though, we were feeling like it was time to move on. This was the first of many places where we felt we stayed one day too long. In retrospect, I actually believe this feeling indicates perfect timing. We were able to leave relaxed but feeling like we hadn't missed a thing.

7. Orange Walk & Lamanai, Belize (Days 39 to 42)

Our return to Orange Walk was refreshing. We caught the bus at 6:30 a.m. and this time did not run out of gas. We were delivered to our (by comparison) luxurious hotel by 8 a.m., where they let us take advantage of the included breakfast even though we weren't even checked in yet. Never ones to turn down free food, we accepted before wandering around town a bit. We'd passed through Orange Walk several times, but this was the first time we'd done more than change buses.

While Sarteneja has the feel of a fledgling tourist destination that isn't exactly sure what to do with the tourists when they actually show up, Orange Walk is a well-worn, comfortable town where tourists pass through regularly, but don't seem to linger. For example, in Orange Walk restaurants and hotels had signs that told us they were restaurants and hotels and looked like they wanted us to stop in. By contrast, in Sarteneja it seemed we had to guess if we were indeed walking into a restaurant or wandering uninvited into someone's kitchen.

We spent four days, alternately exploring town and enjoying the air conditioning and Wi-Fi at our hotel, catching up on some blogging as well as researching and making reservations for the next week of travel to San Ignacio in western Belize and across the Guatemalan border to the Mayan archaeological site of Tikal.

The biggest reason people visit Orange Walk, and our main reason for staying a few days, was the Lamanai Mayan Archaeological Site. When we first visited Belize in 2010, this was one of the things we skipped. This time it was high on my list of must-sees.

Lamanai is unique among Mayan sites for two main reasons:

1. It was continuously inhabited from 1500BC through 1800AD –
that is a seriously long time and means that it continued to be
inhabited several hundred years after many other Mayan sites in
the region had been abandoned. Because Lamanai was built on
a river, the people there were able to avoid drought-related food
and water crises that plagued other cities. In case math is not
your strong suit, I'd like to emphasize the longevity of this
civilization - 1500BC to 1800AD is over 3,000 years! Technically,
it's 3,300 years and the fact that I would round this number to
3,000 alone says something about its magnitude as I'd be

rounding off more time than the United States has even been a country.

2. You get there via a 25-mile boat ride up the New River, which in my opinion is far more fun than a bus or rental car. To ice the proverbial cake there are lots of animals to be seen along the way. The name Lamanai means "submerged crocodile," and I was hoping to see at least one.

On the ride upriver, our guide pointed out spider monkeys, a collection of impressive birds, including what he referred to as a "Jesus bird" for the way it appeared to walk on water as it stepped delicately from lily pad to lily pad, and these amazing little bats plastered almost invisibly to a tree trunk overhanging the river. (I tried to employ Google's help in figuring out what kind of bat they were after the fact, but with over 70 species of bats living in Belize, I quickly gave up.)

We also saw a large rum distillery and got a rather up close view of the huge six-car barge that hauls the sugar cane upriver. As the barge passed within inches of our tiny motorboat, we found ourselves looking 10 feet almost straight up at its iron side.

Once we arrived at Lamanai, we got to see and climb several of the high temples, exploring the nooks and crannies to our hearts' content. To get to the top of the High Temple, it was necessary to climb a series of steep but shallow knee-high steps using a length of rope dangling from somewhere near the top of the steps, where it was presumably mounted securely. It was a steep climb, but at the top, there was a 360-degree view that was well worth the climb. We stood atop the rainforest canopy and looked out over the treetops stretching to the New River Lagoon in the east and away in every other direction to the horizon.

Getting back down was a bit different with the ruins of the city spreading away in every direction hundreds of feet below. I found it best to disregard the rope on the way down and turned to face the temple steps, backing down like on a ladder, slow and steady and focused firmly on my feet. This was not for the faint of heart.

The ruins of the city were the focal point of the trip and were amazing. However, being more biologist than historian, the highlight for me happened shortly after we arrived as we were climbing around on one temple or another. We looked up in the trees and there was a troop of Yucatan black howler monkeys coming down to check us out. (Remember Bean from Sarteneja? Someday she will be this big and self-sufficient.) There were a handful of monkeys of different sizes, including mamas with little ones clinging to their backs or stomachs as they swung effortlessly through the trees alternating between their five prehensile appendages. They were following the trail of tasty leaves through the trees and weren't too concerned by us, coming within 20 feet or so. I could have sat there all day watching them swing and munch.

At this point the day was nearly perfect as far as I was concerned, although I was still holding out hope of seeing a crocodile. On the return trip, I stayed alert, scanning the riverside vegetation and carefully checking that each floating log was not more than it appeared all the way downriver. Unfortunately, it was not to be and I would have to wait months and travel thousands of miles before I finally got to see my first croc.

Getting back to the hotel that night we inventoried our money for the day. We needed dinner and we quickly realized we only had $3US left. Undaunted, we decided we were up for the challenge and headed out. This is when we first discovered the economy and deliciousness of street food. In the evening on the town square, stands of all sorts started popping up. We went in for a closer look and were pleasantly surprised to find garnaches (small fried tortillas topped with refried beans, shredded cabbage, cheese, vinegar and salt) were 4/$1BZ (so 8/$1US) and street tacos were 3/$1BZ. Turns out we ate just fine on our three dollars. And the food was delectable.

In the morning, we discovered that drinkable yogurt was popular, and therefore cheap, and that the local bakery had all kinds of affordable treats. Not just rolls and doughnuts, but breads that could serve as a meal, with meat and cheese baked in. We picked up a tray and a pair of tongs at the door and wandered the bakery taking one of these and one of those. In the end we had trouble controlling our curiosity and ended up with several meals' worth, but it cost just a few dollars. Once we found someone selling bags of those tasty genipes and cashews (which also grow locally), we were set until the evening food stands appeared again.

In addition to exploring ancient Mayan cities and discovering cheap food, Orange Walk was also where we received word that we were officially homeless. That is to say that after remotely navigating seemingly endless negotiations and repairs, our house in Fort Collins was officially under new ownership and we were homeowners no longer. This was a huge relief, but not the cash infusion to our trip or return savings we were hoping for. We'd been hoping to create a bigger cushion for readjustment at the end of our trip or to allow for some "splurges" along the way above our minimal $85 a day budget. In the end, once concessions and repairs were made, the house sold for just a few thousand dollars above what we owed. However, the freedom of no longer having to dread a message from our realtor citing yet another drain to fix or pipe to replace was priceless.

Not having a permanent address was a bit of an adjustment, primarily in a logistical sense. It turns out that our world is not designed for nomads and all kinds of things from credit cards and bank accounts to travel insurance require a valid address, which we no longer had. We ended up using my parents' Pennsylania address for most things, hopeful that this wouldn't mess up our Colorado residency in any significant way.

On the emotional side, this "loss of home" was a somewhat surprising non-issue for me. At this point we were too caught up in the excitement of making the world our home to think too much about the lack of a permanent physical structure. I felt that wherever we were physically, as long as Daryle and I were there together, that was home enough for me.

The next day, we'd be calling the town of San Ignacio in western Belize home, albeit briefly.

8. San Ignacio, Belize, Tikal and Flores, Guatemala (Days 43 to 47)

Getting to San Ignacio required another two bus trips, but both thankfully were on paved roads, and neither involved the siphoning of emergency fuel. We'd ridden the bus to San Ignacio before and we'd booked a room at the same hotel, but I was fascinated by how different the experience felt the second time around.

When we'd arrived on our first trip just two years earlier, I was feeling overwhelmed, out of my element, lost and unmistakably foreign. I felt out of place and awkward, like we were the only tourists and everyone knew it. I was relieved to walk into our hotel and talk to the owner, who was originally from Colorado, and I was happy to have dinner down the street at a popular expat pizza shop. The walk to the pizza shop in the dark unnerved me, but the presence of Americans speaking English and eating familiar food made me feel at home. The especially interesting thing to me now about how relieved I was to see others "like me" is that we'd only been away from home for five days at that point.

The experience this time, five weeks after leaving home, could not have felt more different. It was fun to be back somewhere we'd stayed before, and all the discomfort and nervousness were gone. I didn't feel out of place at all, but welcome and confident. I wanted to wander around and explore. People said hello and I noticed how many other tourists there really were. The town hadn't changed, but I had.

This experience sticks with me as a clear example of how my comfort zone can expand quickly and without my even realizing it. This time San Ignacio was totally within my comfort zone. It was the next part of the journey that was going to stretch me.

I didn't get to revel in my realizations for long, as San Ignacio was only a one-night stopover on this trip. We'd previously hung around several days to explore the jungle, but this time we were headed straight on to Tikal, across the border in northeast Guatemala. Now encompassed within Tikal National Park, the city of Tikal was once home to over 150,000 Mayans. Most visitors to Tikal take a tour either from Flores in Guatemala or San Ignacio in Belize, but we wanted to start in San Ignacio and end up in Flores. We hadn't been able to find a tour to fit that agenda so our planning had been a bit more complicated and ala carte.

We'd read that crossing the border should definitely be done during daylight and that transportation was frequently unreliable. Despite decent bus service in both countries, we couldn't find a single public transport option that would get us directly to Tikal from San Ignacio. We could take the Belize bus to the border, walk across the border and pick up a Guatemalan bus that ran twice a day, but even that plan would take us 19 miles past the road to Tikal and on to the town of Flores. And there was that part about transportation being unreliable. Relying on "two buses a day" seemed like a recipe for getting stranded at the border in the middle of the jungle.

Experiences on our previous trip had led us to believe there was reason to be a bit cautious in the border region. Belize and Guatemala have a troubled history and the border area is fairly remote. Visiting the Mayan ruins of Caracol, in Belize near the Guatemala border for instance, required either an organized tour or that you travel in a police-escorted motorcade that left once a day and returned before dark. When we drove into the jungle on our previous trip to see some amazing caves and waterfalls, we encountered very few tourists but several armed Belizean soldiers on ATVs at every site. We felt completely safe, but it appeared caution was called for.

As usual, I looked at every option I could find for getting us from point A to point B and then started narrowing things down. In the end, I contacted a tour company based in San Ignacio that agreed to shuttle us to Tikal along with one of their tours – if they had space. Luckily for us, it turned out they did. It was pricier than the bus/walk/bus option but would take us exactly where we wanted to go without any changes in transportation, and it was still a fair bit cheaper than an organized tour.

Most encounters with immigration and customs are still out of my comfort zone and since Belize to Guatemala was our first "new-to-us" border crossing, the idea of doing it in a tourist van with a guide rather than alone on foot was also undeniably appealing. We didn't even have to get out of the van at the border. Our guide ran into the guard station with our passports and then returned with them stamped. Easy peasy.

In Tikal, we had booked a room at the only hotel inside the National Park, within walking distance of the ancient city. The location of the hotel was near perfect and our huge room dwarfed our belongings. Although only a single room, it had three full-size beds. We used them all. To my delight, there were also new animals to watch from our doorway, a pool and, best of all, in the morning we could wake up and walk right over to the ruins for a sunrise tour.

The sunrise tour at Tikal was one of the undeniable highlights of our trip. Not huge fans of getting up at 4 a.m., it needs to be something pretty special to make rising this early seem worthwhile to us, and this definitely was. We walked through the deserted city to one of the high temples known as "Pyramid IV" and climbed 198 steps, taking us above the jungle canopy. From there we took a seat on the edge of the temple and watched as daylight crept over the horizon. As the jungle started to wake up, the decibel level climbed. The Howler monkeys and 380 species of birds seemed like they suddenly all had a lot to say. As the sun inched toward the horizon, we started to see the other high temples in the distance peeking above the treetops. The sky was tinged with pink and the mist hung low in the trees, giving the scene a mystical, otherworldly feel.

(Side note for Star Wars fans, Daryle informed me that this is the view you see as the X-wings launch from the Yavin IV rebel base at the end of Episode 4.)

All too soon, sunrise turned to full-on daylight, the magic subsided, and it was time to climb back down below the canopy.

On the walk back through the complex, it was relatively empty, with only the other sunrise tourists rather than the busloads present during the day. It was an added bonus of the sunrise tour to experience the site while it was still peaceful and to have the opportunity to take photos without hordes of people in them.

The daytime cacophony of the jungle continued and our guide pointed out our first flock of parrots. They were beautiful, with their smooth vibrant green feathers and brilliant red and yellow faces. When they opened their beaks, they proved to be some of the loudest contributors to the racket, letting out squawks that far surpassed their relatively small size. Having only seen parrots in the zoo or as pets, it was odd and thrilling to see them in the wild – they hardly seemed real. I am constantly amazed at the variety of brilliant colors and exotic sounds being shown off in the natural world, especially in the tropics.

In the early evening of that same day, we found ourselves trying to track down some howler monkeys in a stand of trees near the hotel. If you haven't heard a howler, they're incredibly loud and you can hear them for miles, making them difficult to locate. The sound they make might have you thinking more of a jaguar than a monkey.

On our first trip to Belize, I had spent an entire night in a screened in cabana in the jungle afraid to take the 100-yard trip to the bathroom because I was sure the noises I heard were coming from a jaguar roaring in the woods nearby. I now know it was a far less threatening troop of howler monkeys.

We finally zeroed in on a handful of trees and could catch some glimpses of the group we had been after, swinging about far up in the branches.

When we got back to the hotel for dinner, I was thrilled to see several "rodents of unusual size" hanging around the hotel eating cashew fruit. The agouti is essentially a really big guinea pig – a guinea pig the size of a large housecat. They eat like squirrels, sitting up on their hind legs and using their front paws to hold the delicious cashew fruits as they munch away. I've read they're quite shy, but as with many animals living near parks and hotels, that wasn't the case here. They probably wouldn't have been fans of my walking out into the yard and attempting to scoop one up for a hug, but they were perfectly content to have us watch them from our doorway several feet away as they hopped around, foraging and nibbling.

In Tikal, our reliance on electricity and internet availability was brought abruptly to our attention. Because we were largely planning the trip as we went, we were researching destinations, downloading maps and communicating with potential hosts daily and Wi-Fi had been a primary qualification when selecting places to stay on our trip thus far. Not only were we reliant on the internet, but on power in general, to charge laptops, phones and camera batteries. Given the small amount of luggage we were carrying, we had a surprising number of electronic devices.

As I mentioned, our hotel in Tikal was very nice, clean, modern and roomy. And they were technically correct in advertising that they had Wi-Fi. What wasn't mentioned on their website, or in any obvious way at the hotel itself, was that they had power only via generator and only for a few hours each evening, from roughly 8 to 10 p.m.

We suddenly realized how much we took power and internet for granted and this was a wake-up call letting us know we could get ourselves in trouble down the road if we didn't learn to mitigate this reliance. There are few things more disappointing when traveling than showing up to a once-in-a-lifetime sight without a functioning camera or more unnerving than arriving in one of the world's largest cities with no place to stay.

After two nights in Tikal, we hopped on a shuttle to the nearby tourist town of Flores. We spent two days exploring and, most memorably, discovering more lessons in how to find the best food. Initially, we found Flores to be frustratingly expensive. We'd set our overall budget for the trip at $85/day, but lowered that to $50/day for Central America in order to save up for the months we planned to spend in Europe later in the trip. Although we'd found a hotel in Flores for $18US a night, when we went in search of dinner, we found restaurant after restaurant where we would easily have spent $20-$30 on dinner for the two of us, without even including drinks. Since that wasn't in our budget, we kept walking and began to notice a pattern. All of these restaurants had menus, in English, posted outside their doors. We realized we needed to figure out where the Guatemalans ate.

Eventually, we found a plaza full of carts, each with a Guatemalan woman serving homemade food to dozens of Guatemalans lined up and filling the plaza – sitting on stairs, benches and anywhere there was a flat space. It looked like a community potluck. We had found the holy grail of dining on the road. We got in line, pointed to some appetizing items and for $2.50 we had all we could want. Then we found more carts with desserts and despite being full already, spent another $1.25 on a bag of fresh mango and some pastries. Instead of eating overpriced versions of what Guatemalans thought tourists might want to eat, we got to eat what actual Guatemalans eat. Some were new things we'd never seen or tasted before and many were things we couldn't exactly identify. Trying new food is hands down one of my favorite parts of travel and this was a perfect evening in that regard.

From Flores, we were headed to the eastern part of Guatemala, to the city of Chiquimula. This was the opposite direction from most tourists, who go west to beautiful Lake Atitlán and the popular city of Antigua with its numerous Spanish language schools. We were about to venture off the beaten path.

Because of things we'd read, we were a bit concerned about getting safely from Flores to Chiquimula, where we'd be met by friends of friends. It was a long distance and we needed to take a bus. What we'd read advised us to "avoid low-priced public intra- and inter-city buses … Public buses are subject to frequent attacks by armed robbers and often are poorly maintained and dangerously driven." Interesting, we thought, and proceeded to ask our soon-to-be hosts for the names of the most reputable bus lines. We also decided to take a trip to the local bus station on a recon mission the day before we left.

When we arrived at the station in our tuk-tuk (a three-wheeled vehicle used as a taxi, common in Central America and Asia), we knew better than to hesitate and made a beeline for the station doors. In developing countries, it seemed as if every moment of idleness indicated indecisive weakness. Stand still for just a moment and we'd find ourselves surrounded by an ever-increasing horde of local businessmen, ticket-sellers and taxi drivers, each insisting we needed their product or service so loudly we couldn't hear ourselves think. We'd experienced this in Mexico and again in Belize, where we had allowed ourselves to be pressured into what turned out to be a completely unnecessary three block cab ride, just because we exited the bus station without knowing precisely where we were or where we were going. We found it all too easy to get flustered and overwhelmed by the sensory overload so we had learned to compare notes and make sure we had an agreed upon plan of attack before setting foot outside a cab or transport station. We have found there will almost always still be taxis, tours and tickets available later, and sometimes it's best to walk straight past the crazy, regroup, and come back if need be. As much as we were learning, it seemed there was still always one unexpected twist to trip us up.

Once inside the bus terminal, we looked around and saw a number of ticket windows at the far end of the hall with other small offices lining the walls along the way. We headed straight for one of the distant ticket windows, but before we made it far, we were approached by a man from one of the small offices offering to sell us the bus tickets we needed. We determined that he had tickets to the bus line and route we wanted at the price we expected so we followed him to his office, where we purchased tickets for the next day. He told us to return to his office ahead of our departure time and stressed repeatedly that we should come directly to his office when we arrived at the station.

When we arrived the next day, we checked in with our guy, and even though we could see the clearly marked waiting area where dozens of other passengers were waiting for their respective buses, he insisted we needed to wait in his office. This seemed odd, but not dangerous, so we went in and took a seat. We sat there for 15 minutes, then half an hour as our departure time approached, watching the movements in the station through the glass walls. We heard an announcement for a bus boarding that sounded strangely like our bus, but he assured us it was a different bus. We didn't believe him, but still we stayed. Looking at Daryle, I could see my own anxiety mirrored in his eyes. What had we gotten ourselves into? Was our bus about to leave without us?

All this time, our ticket seller was communicating by phone, arranging unknown things in rapid Spanish, which I couldn't exactly make out but gathered had to do with us. The bus we thought might be ours departed and still we sat, increasingly uneasy. Then, abruptly, we were rushed out to a waiting shuttle van which we were told would "take us to our bus, which left from another place." We were initially nervous as the van pulled out of the station with only us, a driver and the ticket seller on board, but we quickly found ourselves closely following the bus that had just departed from the station.

We followed close behind the bus until we were a mile or two from the station. Then we watched fascinated and a bit perplexed, as the bus pulled over, followed by our van. Relieved, we got out, got on the bus, handed over our tickets and found seats. We watched as the guy who sold us the tickets handed over some money to the bus driver.

Judging by the lack of response or emotion from the other passengers, this was not an uncommon occurrence. In the end, it worked out fine and I don't even think we got ripped off. I think the bus company probably did and that the ticket guy and the bus driver made some extra cash, but we got where we were going safe and sound at a reasonable price, albeit with some unnecessary anxiety.

There were so many times on this journey that we thought, "I have no idea what is going on here" or "I am trusting this stranger to be who they said and to do what they promised." But you know what? Things always worked out, people always came through, and we gradually learned that the very best travel advice we had ever received came from a tour guide on our first-ever trip out of the country, six years earlier. It probably wasn't even meant as advice, but more of an exhortation to a van full of uptight American tourists to relax and trust him, but it stuck.

We were staying at an all-inclusive resort in the Yucatan back in 2006 and had chosen to go on a guided tour to the Mayan site of Coba to get out and see a few things outside the hotel. As we hurtled down the shoulder of a Mexican highway in a tour van, passing cars on the right, our tour guide, Jorge, urged us calmly in heavily accented English, "Don't freak out!"

It sounds like a small thing, but this simple phrase became a rallying cry in my daily life and carried us though many nerve-wracking moments on our trip. Daryle and I found ourselves repeating the immortal words of Jorge frequently on this journey as we looked at each other with a secret shared smile, and never once did his advice ever let us down.

9. Chiquimula, Guatemala (Days 48 to 49)

The bus debacle was just the beginning of a very long day. The reason we were headed to Chiquimula in the first place (and the reason we were the only tourists on the bus) is that the Rotary Club I belonged to in Colorado had partnered on several occasions with a club in Chiquimula and another in the nearby city of Gualan. While we were traveling, Daryle and I wanted to take the opportunity to see some of the projects that members of my club had made possible both financially, and by getting their hands dirty on the ground alongside their Guatemalan counterparts.

Rotary is an international service organization founded in 1905 and made up of over 35,000 Rotary Clubs in more than 200 countries. Members of these clubs are community and business leaders who are committed to creating a better world by working together.

Clubs partner on projects that generally focus on enhancing education and job training, providing clean water, combating hunger, improving health and sanitation, or eradicating disease. Worldwide there is an amazing collection of noteworthy projects pursued by the 1.2 million members of Rotary.

Knowing that there are groups of people around the world individually and collectively committed to the Rotary motto of "service above self" is in itself incredibly encouraging to me. I was excited to receive my first chance to experience first-hand some of the joint projects between a U.S. club and a club in a developing nation.

The way international service works in Rotary is that clubs with an excess of resources partner with clubs with an excess of needs. In this way, the resources are directed to the needs of a community, identified by those who live there rather than perceived by others from afar. Both clubs put in time, money and resources, and through all phases of the project there are people nearby invested in and overseeing the work to make sure the actual needs of the people are being addressed in a sustainable way.

In addition to wanting to see an effective Rotary partnership firsthand, we knew that having a local host would be an ideal way to make Guatemala more approachable for us and to more deeply experience the country and learn about its people.

For these reasons, we found ourselves on a bus to Chiquimula, expecting to be picked up by strangers, but strangers to whom we were remotely connected. We would be met by relatives of the couple we'd be staying with when we arrived in Chiquimula. These relatives, however, did not speak English.

I had been avoiding phone calls requiring communication in Spanish thus far by using email and text, and I had been relying heavily on ample thinking time and Google Translate to compose even those brief messages. I don't really enjoy talking on the phone to begin with, but talking to a stranger in a foreign language was an especially intimidating notion to me. I'd put it off as long as possible, but we'd been texting with the couple who would be picking us up over several hours on the bus ride and there was some confusion about where we needed to get off the bus to meet them. It had become increasingly obvious that a phone call was going to be necessary, and when they asked me to give them a call, I took a deep breath and made the call.

Like many things, the phone call turned out to be less scary and less of a big deal than I'd made it out in my mind, and I proved more capable than I'd given myself credit for. I figured out that we needed to get off the bus before it made the turn into town rather than waiting for the station. This was a long-distance bus, not one with frequent stops, so I had to not only explain the location to the bus driver but also convince him to make an early stop for us. Each piece of this adventure was stressful in itself, but cumulatively it was exhausting, and there was no sharing the load or passing the buck on this one. Daryle spoke about five words of Spanish – hola, gracias, adios, bueno, cerveza – so all Spanish communication fell to me.

We succeeded in getting off at the right intersection and when we were greeted by our new friends, I felt a brief, but significant sense of satisfaction with my communication achievement. The day was only half over though and I continued to press on, struggling to hold up my end of a polite conversation on the drive.

For anyone who has been suddenly dumped into a language immersion situation, you know it takes a surprising amount of mental energy to navigate. I had to remind myself that this discomfort and stretching is part of why I travel, and that next time we were in a similar situation it wouldn't be quite so overwhelming. Over and over on our trip I noticed how quickly my brain recognized a situation I'd encountered before, even if only once, and deemed it familiar and as having no cause for fear or anxiety, allowing me to smoothly handle situations that were previously paralyzing. However, that knowledge was little help as I continued to struggle for words.

About 30 minutes down the road, we stopped at a steakhouse where our new friends bought us the biggest lunch I've ever seen. We heard all over the world about the magnitude of "American portion sizes," and there is certainly some truth to it, but based on this experience, we have nothing on Guatemala. It was about 2:30 in the afternoon by this point and not knowing when we would have our next meal, we'd already eaten lunch once on the bus ride. I tried to find something relatively light-looking on the menu and settled on a tuna salad.

When it arrived, it turned out to be mostly an unimpressive pile of canned tuna whipped up with mayonnaise on a bed of lettuce. What captivated my attention immediately though were the four whole avocados sliced in half and ringing the plate. I've eaten an entire avocado in one sitting and felt that was a pretty substantial accomplishment, but four?! I had to wonder what the avocado salad that had also been on the menu looked like.

Everyone shared food from their massive plates with us as well, and once we were stuffed to American Thanksgiving proportions, we waddled back to the car and drove the rest of the way to our host's home.

Verónica and her husband greeted us enthusiastically and gave us a little time to settle into our rooftop room and grab a siesta. Shortly though, she came to let us know that they had some friends who'd like to meet us. In fact, these friends were already downstairs and they were going to have dinner with us. Dinner? But we just ate dinner! A lot of dinner! Not wanting to be rude, we prepared to eat as much as we could. Being in Guatemala was like going home with my college roommate from rural North Carolina for the weekend. We had arrived at 9 p.m. and yet there was a meal with ten different dishes on the table. No one ever wanted us to be hungry and all weekend, I heard "That's all you're going to have? Don't you want some more?" I'm not a light eater and I can put away some food, but there are limits.

However, we loved our hosts and the new friends, Lorena & Oscar, who'd come over to meet us and after dinner we headed to a local bar where a band was playing classic rock hits. Our new friends requested "Hotel California" for us and we had to laugh. We'd read that this is a song you will hear all over the world. It seems to be the song most commonly associated with Americans. We especially enjoyed the bands manual reverb echo, repeating the last syllable over and over a bit quieter each time. They used this technique a lot and it made us laugh every time. Welcome to the Hotel California –a –a-a-a-a.

In the morning, we woke up to what Daryle felt was the strangest food we ate on the entire trip. Rice Krispies served with warm milk. (It's important to remember that it was about 100 degrees every day we were in Chiquimula and there was no A/C, so warmth would not necessarily be something you were looking to add to a food. (Now, ice cream dipped in Rice Krispies? There you might have had something.) I suspect the oddness of the food may have been lost on me, because as we were eating breakfast, our host unexpectedly asked me if I'd be willing to say a few words at "la oracion" we were heading to after breakfast.

We were going to see a water project that our respective Rotary Clubs had partnered on, and I gathered there was going to be a little presentation. As a representative of my Club, I didn't really feel I had a choice. Besides feeling rude, no matter how politely I declined, I knew I'd only be shying away because I was afraid. So, I said yes, followed by "this is going to have to be in Spanish isn't it?" I spent the rest of breakfast jotting down notes in Spanish and having Verónica edit them, until I had a short paragraph prepared, thanking everyone involved, talking about how great this was for the health and education of the children in the villages, how wonderful it was to get to be there, etc.

Although Chiquimula was a modern city of about 80,000, the water project was in a neighboring village that was surprisingly rural and that had significantly fewer resources. Despite the short distance (it took us only 45 minutes to drive there), the winding roads and steep mountains made the town feel far more isolated than expected.

Before this project, the local school had no running water. Every day, time had to be dedicated to fetching water for drinking and handwashing rather than to studying. The completion of this project was a big deal for this community and as we got out of the car and started looking around, I realized this gathering was of more consequence than I'd realized. I had figured it would be primarily members of the local Rotary Club, probably 30 at most. Once we arrived it was apparent that the Chiquimula Rotarians were the least of the guests in terms of number. There were hundreds of residents of the local communities utilizing the school; members of the construction and engineering committees; and even the mayor ("el jefe") of Chiquimula. There were several rows of plastic chairs set out in the middle of a field facing a space with a lone microphone.

After mingling and being introduced to and chatting with other local Rotary members and honored guests, I was shown to a seat in the front row, next to El Jefe. I started to sweat. Rotary members and guests filled the remaining seats and most of the locals gathered around in groups to stand around the edges or sit on the ground. As the presentation started, I did my best to stay focused and pick out enough words to know when I was up.

I was pretty sure I'd just heard the "emcee" announce me and as I started to get up, I looked over to Verónica and the other Rotarians, already standing up front, for confirmation. Instead of the "come here" gesture I was expecting, what I saw was more of a shooing, "get out of here" motion. Now I was really confused and I froze, halfway out of my seat. Everyone was watching me. I looked over again; more adamant shooing this time. Their faces, however, looked like they were urging me on, while their hands were shooing me away. I decided to go with the encouraging faces and started to walk forward. They seemed relieved, so I was also relieved. It seemed I had chosen correctly.

To this point, gestures and nonverbal communication in the places we'd visited had been pretty identical and there was no indication up to this point that there would be any significant challenges in Guatemala. I would never have guessed the hand signals would throw me off; you never know when there will be a sudden and unexpected breakdown in communication.

I went up to accept a certificate on behalf of my Rotary Club and read my prepared speech. There were no looks of confusion and it seemed that at least the majority of guests had understood what I was trying to convey. I breathed a sigh of relief and took my seat again.

After the formal recognition and speech-giving, we went to a spigot where El Jefe and I ceremonially turned on the water and many photos were taken. This was an amazing experience. It was odd to be the representative, because my only direct involvement in the project itself was being there that day. However, I knew it was meaningful for the community to have a real, live representative from the Colorado club that had been instrumental in the realization of this community development project and it was an honor to fill that role.

After the official ceremony, it was lunch time. As the honored guests, we and the Chiquimula Rotary members were shown to a lone pair of tables in the middle of the field where we were served chicken, a variety of salads and tortillas – more than we could eat. Meanwhile, the dozens of people from the villages sat around in groups and looked on. I kept looking around at the others eating with us for signs of discomfort, or "this is odd," and saw absolutely none, so I kept chatting, eating and feeling uncomfortable.

Once we were done, we saw all the people who'd been lingering, watching and hanging out start gathering in groups around men with large cardboard boxes. These men then reached into the boxes and started handing out what turned out to be bologna sandwiches. As everyone scattered to find seats on the ground to eat their sandwiches, it was crystal clear to even the most naïve (us) that we were the honored guests. I watched with fascination while continuing to feel even more conspicuous and self-conscious, if that was possible.

When I had started the day, I thought maybe warm Rice Krispies would be the most extraordinary thing I'd encounter. I had no idea what was in store. From visiting a remote village in Guatemala, to giving a speech in Spanish in front of hundreds of strangers, to being the honored guests at the ribbon-cutting of a life-changing project, this easily became one of the most memorable days of my life thus far.

Most remarkable to me is that I didn't make any of it happen, I did nothing more than show up and say yes. Sometimes I guess that's all there is to do.

10. Gualan/Santiago, Guatemala (Days 50 to 52)

That afternoon, after returning from the water project dedication and packing our things, we were driven an hour up the road by Saul, a grey-haired Rotarian and retired teacher. I was pretty pleased with my progress in conversational Spanish by this point and chatted away most of the trip, with no incredibly awkward pauses or impasses in communication. However, when Saul stopped and led us into a gas station to get a Coke, he made a comment about another kind of coke associated with Central America. Caught off guard, I'm sure I had a look of confused shock on my face, not sure whether he could possibly be serious. I didn't really know this man after all. Then he burst out laughing. Relieved, I joined in. Jokes are one of the easiest things to get lost in translation.

We were a little confused overall at this point, which was pretty par for the course. We expected this stop to be a sort of half-way-point handoff, but when Salvador, our new host, showed up he drove us less than a half-mile to his home just around the corner. It turned out the gas station wasn't an arbitrary meeting point but a business owned by Salvador and his wife Milvia. On the short drive to the house, we passed numerous fences and several guards positioned strategically and armed with semiautomatic weapons. There was no explanation from our host, which we'd generally found to mean that there was nothing out of the ordinary to explain, but I was suddenly paying very close attention. It seemed our move from city life in Chiquimula to more rural living came with some unexpected changes. Salvador & his wife, Milvia, had a large and very nice home with significant property, but nothing I would have thought necessitated the security I'd just seen. I was reminded that I wasn't in the U.S. and as much as seemed similar, there was much I didn't know or understand about my surroundings.

I've since learned this type of security probably isn't uncommon, having read accounts of successful avocado farmers in Mexico who've been kidnapped by drug cartels for ransom and even of an entire town that has set up their own heavily armed "avocado police" who patrol the area to protect the town's citizens and farmers from these cartel-related risks. Central America is a relatively narrow funnel through which a large quantity of illegal drugs pass each year on their way to the U.S., putting ordinary law-abiding citizens in the path at potential risk – risk which those with means choose reasonably to mitigate as they can.

Almost as soon as we were out of the car, Salvador asked, "Do you like mangoes?" We could hardly believe our good luck. In our humble opinion, mangoes are quite possibly the most delicious food on the planet. "We absolutely love mangoes," we replied with huge excited smiles.

Based on the few really good mangoes Daryle and I had managed to sample prior to our trip, we knew they had the potential to be amazing, and we'd been sampling local fresh mangoes as much as possible since day one in mango country back on April 1 in Sayulita. However, Daryle had been constantly thwarted on his mission to eat a mango straight from the tree.

It seemed rather serendipitous that, only moments after arriving, Salvador presented us with not just the opportunity to eat a mango from a tree, but many mangoes directly from many trees.

Salvador proceeded to lead us out to his yard where he had his gardener pick one after another kind of mango, along with a few other fruits we'd never tasted. We then sat on the patio carving and slurping up the most delicious fruit imaginable until we were sticky up to our elbows and could eat no more. Then, bellies full of mangoes, we learned that it was time to go to a Rotary meeting, with a robust dinner. Does the food never end? we wondered.

The next day we toured a health facility where my Rotary Club had collaborated on several projects specifically addressing the prevention of Dengue fever, a mosquito-borne virus found in the tropics that can result in serious illness. There had obviously been huge improvements in the medical facilities here, but as we looked around it was impossible not to compare what we saw with what we were used to in terms of what a medical facility looks and feels like.

One of the areas where the clinic was looking to make some improvements was its maternity ward. As we were shown around, I couldn't help thinking about my expectations for medical care in general, and a maternity ward specifically. What I was looking at in Guatemala made it clear that in many places in the world, expectations are different. Mothers are happy to have a basic, clean place lie down and trained staff to help with the delivery.

I have to say I was surprised to see that even in a facility partnered with Rotary, and therefore presumably receiving above-average support and improvements, the standards were a world away from what I would personally consider even marginally acceptable back home.

There were no private rooms, no air conditioning. The walls and floors were stained, the sheets threadbare, the mattresses thin. Perhaps most importantly, there was no access to basic equipment for emergency resuscitation of newborns, which we learned would go a long way in decreasing the infant mortality rate.

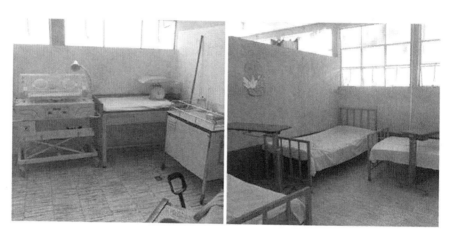

Our visit to this clinic had a powerful impact on me. I had expected more. I thought about all my friends back in Colorado who had given birth in the past few years, and whom I thought would be horrified to see the conditions that women in much of the world experience.

Beyond that I thought about all the expectations I have about my world and the resources that I expect to be available to me. I was reminded of the thousands of things that I take for granted on a regular basis – that I can go to a doctor or hospital for care and they will have the resources to take care of me; that when I go to the store, there will be food on the shelves; that when I turn on a faucet, there will be water I can drink. This is a theme I'd return to so many times on this trip when my basic first-world expectations were violated.

The reality is that my temporary inconvenience is someone else's way of life, not by choice, but by necessity. I believe this realization is an example of the crucial impact of travel on worldview. As they say, "You don't know what you don't know." But once you do know, you can't forget.

Later that evening we had an unexpected chance to take a peek inside an intimate part of Guatemalan culture. Salvador's family had lived in this area for hundreds of years. In fact, we'd had a long discussion about how rooted he felt in this community and how hard it was for him to understand why we would want to sell everything and leave our home as we had. It seemed like he knew everyone. He knew about their family. He checked in on people. He seemed like an important guy, so we weren't surprised when he told us there was a wake he and Milvia needed to attend that evening. What did surprise us was that he invited us to join them. Initially we wavered, afraid we might feel out of place, but then reasoned that if it wasn't appropriate for us to attend, he wouldn't have invited us. Thinking this was probably a once-in-a-lifetime kind of opportunity, we accepted.

While on the way, Salvador mentioned there would be coffee and that it "may be too strong" for us. This struck us as curious. We are no strangers to strong coffee, but we didn't give it much thought.

We spent several hours outside the family home, sitting in folding chairs, surrounded by hundreds of community members.

As the sun set, we were served coffee and cookies by the family. The coffee was indeed very strong, and drinking it as the sun went down was an odd juxtaposition for someone who conservatively shies away from caffeine after noon.

The immediate family was inside the house with the body and, illustrating why it's called a wake, and why strong coffee was such a key part of the proceedings, some of these people would indeed stay up all night with the family to watch over the body of the deceased until burial the following day. Thankfully, Salvador and Milvia weren't in that category, and after several hours when it started to rain a bit, we headed home.

As I look back from my present perspective as someone who again has a "regular" job and whose days slip by quickly, as barely distinguishable replicas of one another, I'm repeatedly amazed at how many unique experiences we routinely had in such relatively short periods of time on this trip. We only spent 48 hours with Salvador and Milvia and yet we had many discussions and experiences that I still think about today and have spent months processing.

Most days I loved this excitement of meeting new people, having new experiences and being "on the move," but occasionally it was a real drag.

Instead of sleeping much on that final night in Santiago, I spent several hours relieving my stomach of its contents. It is unpleasant enough to do this in your own home, but in the home of someone you've only just met, I found it excruciatingly uncomfortable. Vomiting quietly, it turns out, is challenging and I just hoped our hosts were sound sleepers.

The next morning, I woke up wanting nothing more than to pull the covers over my head and sleep another hour or four, but it was a travel day and we were scheduled to take a bus and a water taxi to our next destination, several hours to the northwest where we had a hotel reservation waiting for us.

I'm sure you've heard the phrase, "Life is a journey, not a destination," and I know I am not the first nor will I be the last to cite that quote in a travel book. However, there are some days in life and in travel when enjoying the journey is harder than others, and you just wish you'd get to the damn destination already. This was one of those days.

At breakfast, I tried to gracefully explain in my mediocre Spanish that I wasn't feeling particularly well and wasn't all that hungry. As a guest though, I still felt obligated to eat the meal graciously put before me. Needless to say, the deep-fried tortilla-based meal did not sit especially well. I persevered, and after breakfast we repacked our bags and Salvador drove us to the bus station. An excellent host to the end, he didn't just drop us off, but waited nearly an hour with us until our bus arrived and we boarded before getting back in his truck and heading home.

Within half an hour of departing the station, we witnessed an impressive display of self-sufficiency, teamwork and resourcefulness. We'd barely left town on our three-hour journey to Puerto Barrios when we came to a sudden and unexpected stop. Not slow creeping traffic; this was the complete-cessation-of-movement kind of traffic jam. For another half hour, we wondered what was happening. (Although I'll be honest, as someone who gets motion sick even when not already ill, I was thrilled to remain stationary for a few minutes.) When we finally crept past the bottleneck, what we saw was 10 or 15 Guatemalans, machetes in hand, hacking away at a very sizeable tree that most likely toppled in the previous night's rainstorm. In the half hour we sat there, these guys had managed to remove this huge tree from the road, piece by piece using only machetes.

If you need something done here, like the removal of a large tree from the road, I suspect you can't wait around for the department of transportation to come along and take care of it in a timely manner. I am certain these 10-15 gentlemen were just the first ones on the scene, and they knew if they wanted to get through they'd need to take care of it themselves, so they jumped out and started hacking. From what I could tell, pretty much every man in rural Guatemala had a machete within arm's reach, at all times. It's a pretty essential tool for life in rural Central America, as we saw in this example, but, like the armed guards at Salvador's, it takes an adjustment to get used to seeing men everywhere casually wearing machetes in a belt holster.

The rest of the bus ride was uneventful and beautiful as we wound through a gorgeous green forested slice of Guatemalan countryside. I savored my time alone and focused on settling my stomach.

In Puerto Barrios, another incredibly gracious family (relatives of friends of Verónica, our Chiquimula host) picked us up at the bus station, showed us around town, took us home for lunch (of course) and then dropped us off for a half-hour boat ride in a rather small motorboat/water taxi.

Livingston is uniquely located at the mouth of the Rio Dulce and across the Bay of Amantique from the southern tip of Belize. Despite being solidly part of the mainland, the town is accessible only by boat – either from Puerto Barrios, the town of Rio Dulce up the river of the same name, or from Punta Gorda in southern Belize.

At the boat terminal, not feeling any better, I prepared for the upcoming ride as much as possible mentally and by practicing Spanish phrases that might be helpful, such as, "Disculpe, por favor puedo tener este asiento. Possible necessito vomitar." (Translation: "Excuse me, but can I please have this seat. I may need to vomit.")

Once on board and in motion, I had little time to be sick as I had other things to focus on, like survival. I was pretty certain I could feel my brain rattling against my skull and the hull bend under my feet as we hurtled along the surface of the ocean just off the coast, skipping over waves in our tiny boat.

It was a rough day. In the end though, we did make it to Livingston, our final Guatemalan destination, where an incredibly accommodating guest house owner made me a fresh fruit smoothie and I collapsed into bed. I had made it and that felt like a major accomplishment.

11. Livingston, Guatemala (Days 53 to 58)

Our time in Guatemala was characterized by the overwhelming graciousness of strangers. Guatemalans in general and Rotarians in particular had been incredibly friendly and welcoming. Nearly everyone we passed on the street greeted us. We were hosted and treated as friends by people we had never met, based solely on a few emails or phone calls from a mutual friend. And we weren't just welcomed, housed, and fed – as if that weren't enough – these new friends went out of their way to share their country and community with us, connect us with others at our upcoming destinations and make sure we got where we needed to go, even if they had to take us there themselves.

While we were unendingly grateful for the experiences we'd had and people we'd met in Guatemala to this point, disembarking the water taxi in Livingston and getting to our guest house was also an incredible relief. Meeting and staying with locals may be one of my favorite ways to travel, and I believe one of the best ways to really experience a new place, but there are drawbacks as well. Being accountable to someone every minute, staying constantly on our toes, never knowing what was coming next and constantly contending with the language barrier had been exhausting. Once we'd checked into our guest house, I appreciated that I had no feelings of guilt or obligation as I slept for the rest of the day – and most of the next.

After two days of recuperating, I'd regained enough energy to go on the hunt for a new hotel. As accommodating and kind as the owner of our guest house had been, that didn't change the fact that it was about 100 degrees in our room all the time, even with the help of the ceiling fan and an open window.

It had been ridiculously hot for weeks and we had been managing fine without air conditioning so far, but it had not been hot like this. Perhaps when our new friends in Puerto Barrios had been incredibly concerned that we'd chosen a hotel without air conditioning at our next destination, it should have served as a warning. We were apparently and unwittingly now in the hottest part of Guatemala at the hottest time of year. We eventually learned that you ignore the advice of locals at your own peril, but it took a while.

In addition to the temperature, we were sharing a single bathroom with six other guests, a single occupancy kind of bathroom that included the shower. Not feeling well, I had been really nervous that this lack of quick access could work out very badly. I'd made it this long but didn't want to tempt fate.

Luckily, those Puerto Barrios hosts we mentioned that were so concerned that we'd chosen a hotel without air conditioning hadn't only voiced their concern, within 15 minutes of meeting us, they'd also made several phone calls and compiled a short list of hotel recommendations. This is a good example of the amazing hospitality we experienced in Guatemala.

On that hotel short list had been a place called "Hotel Hill," at least that's what we had heard and written down. After breakfast, we set out in search of this "Hotel Hill". After a thorough perusal of town, we had found no establishment by that name, however, we did discover a place called Gil's Resort coincidentally located on the only hill in town. We admitted Hill and Gil could certainly sound similar, especially in Spanish-accented English. We asked to see a room and when we found it had both air conditioning and a ceiling fan, we booked it immediately. It was significantly more expensive than our initial guest house, but it had been so hot and humid for the past month that the air conditioning alone was enough to sell me at this point. Being sick had pushed me way out of my comfort zone and my commitment to the daily travel budget was seriously compromised. I needed air conditioning.

A few hours later we were trekking up the hill to Gil's with our gear, dreaming of a cool reprieve. However, when we arrived and were shown to our room, it was quickly explained to us that there was no power at the moment and therefore the heavenly air conditioning we'd been shown just hours earlier was no longer functional. I was exhausted, drenched in sweat and quite honestly wanted to sit down and cry.

We were pretty sure we understood our new host to say that the power was out in "todo el pueblo" (the whole town), meaning it wouldn't have mattered what hotel we chose, there would be no power, nor air conditioning. We really hoped we also correctly understood them to say it would probably be back on soon.

A later conversation with our previous guest house owner led us to believe power outages were not only common, but could last for several days.

We chose to be optimistic and in the meantime unpacked our bathing suits to take a walk to the tiny beach we'd seen nearby, hoping to find relief from the heat in a different way. Unfortunately, the water was a least as warm as the air. Sigh.

Much to our relief, the electricity did return several hours later, making a good night's sleep finally possible. I was pretty much recovered health-wise by this point and we decided that the next day we would visit a hostel that was located several miles up the Rio Dulce. Exploring online it sounded like we could visit for the day even if we weren't staying there, so we arranged for the owner to pick us up in town the following morning.

The boat trip up the river was beautiful, with steep cliffs peeking through the dense tropical vegetation lining both sides of the river.

There were elegant white egrets perched along the banks and a number of tiny rustic homes with thatched roofs built out of planks and the trunks of small trees.

We heard the calls of monkeys and hundreds of birds as we zipped upriver in our tiny boat. We rented what looked like a hand-dug wooden canoe from the hostel and made the surprisingly difficult paddle upstream to Agua Caliente, a very roughly constructed hot springs pool partially separated from the river by a concrete wall and accessible by a small wooden ladder.

I enjoyed a swim and an unexpectedly close look at some of the local wildlife when an Armageddon-sized grasshopper landed at my feet. It was beautiful, brightly-colored and at least four inches long. Things get really huge in the tropics, especially the insects!

Livingston was another town like Sarteneja, quiet and laid back with not a lot to do. We again timed our stay perfectly, staying six nights but being ready to leave in five.

We spent our last day wandering, reading, writing and generally killing time. Daryle took advantage of the time to get his first haircut of the trip at a small, open-air barber shop. I admit to being a little jealous that all he needed to communicate was "clippers #1" to get a decent haircut.

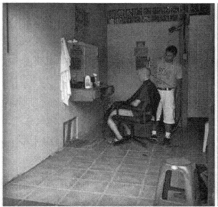 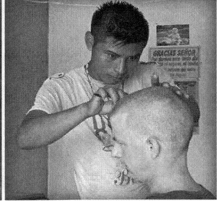

The next morning, we were up early for our water taxi back to Belize. As we stood on the pier, we snapped a few photos of ourselves looking out over the calm expanse of water. There were some significant bands of clouds out over the ocean but we didn't give them a second thought.

The trip we were about to embark on was an hour and a half across the bay and looking out over the water in the direction we knew Belize to be, there was no sign of land. Since this water taxi was only scheduled to run twice a week and traveled across what was essentially open ocean, we were expecting something larger than the small launch we'd taken for the half-hour trip along the coast from Puerto Barrios a week earlier.

When the taxi arrived, we were disappointed to see that it was indeed the same water taxi. About 18 feet long, it had four bench seats that could accommodate a cozy four to five people across. Our transportation staff consisted of a spotter standing in the front and a driver in the back, steering by outboard motor positioning. All luggage was piled in the hull behind the spotter, on top of all the life jackets, which were undoubtedly required to be on board, but apparently not required to be accessible to the passengers. Although there was never a time you couldn't see land on either the Guatemala or Belize side, that land was way out on the horizon and never visible in both directions simultaneously.

We weren't far from shore when it started to rain. Our crew handed out some blue tarps that we stretched across the row on our laps and pulled up over our faces to protect ourselves from the pelting rain as we sped across the bay at top speed. The tarp served a second key purpose, which was to allow us to cover our eyes so we didn't have to see the huge waves that were building around our boat. Periodically the usually loud outboard motor would suddenly fall silent, as the boat went completely airborne and the propellers left the water. At several points, the spotter made a quick hand signal causing the driver to immediately cut the engine, leaving us bobbing around, looking at the huge waves rolling toward us. We're not sure why we stopped, but we were relieved when the motor revved up and we started cutting through the waves again instead of rising and falling on every swell. With waves this tall and a boat this small and light, it seemed that hitting one wave at the wrong angle. more parallel than perpendicular, could launch us into the air and flip us completely. I found myself wondering if the boat would sink slowly enough to extricate a life jacket before it went down. As Belize finally came into view, I made constant mental calculations about whether I thought we were close enough to swim to shore if necessary. Once we were well within that range, I relaxed a little.

This might have been the longest hour and a half of my life and was easily the most terrifying experience of our entire trip. When we made it to Punta Gorda in Belize, we kissed the ground in gratitude and went to find coffee and breakfast. Punta Gorda, like many places in Belize, was far smaller and less commercialized than we expected but we found both coffee and breakfast in what looked less like a restaurant and more like my grandmother's kitchen. In fact, one of the mugs our coffee was served in was identical to one I'd grown up seeing in my grandma's cupboard.

There were a few suggestions rather than a menu per se. We weren't feeling picky or much like making a decision, so we took whatever was suggested, some scrambled eggs with cheese and a muffin as I recall. After getting food and coffee in us, we were feeling mostly recovered from the tense journey and as ready as we were likely to get for taking another bus and another (hopefully much tamer) water taxi. The upcoming taxi was called the Hokey Pokey Water Taxi, seeming to suggest a much more enjoyable ride.

12. Placencia, Belize (Days 59 to 62)

The bus ride from Punta Gorda to the town of Mango Creek was uneventful and the lagoon crossed by the Hokey Pokey Water Taxi was well-protected by the Placencia peninsula and therefore blissfully calm. When we docked in Placencia, we were met by our host, Jeff, at the water taxi terminal and walked the few blocks to his house, a typical Belizean abode adorned in pastel purple and green.

We had met Jeff through Couchsurfing.org. Although we hadn't contacted any Couchsurfers directly to make specific requests for a place to stay in Placencia we had made a general post of our itinerary to our profile. Jeff had seen our plans and reached out to offer his spare room. We wound up staying for five nights. Not only did Jeff provide us a free place to stay (a set of bunk beds in our own room), but we got an insider's experience of Placencia.

Jeff was originally from the United States but had settled in Belize several years prior. He took us on a tour of all his favorite places for food and drink, introducing us to the owners who were all friends and mostly Americans who'd also relocated to the tropics.

Our week in Placencia was incredibly relaxing and we quickly felt at home. We adopted Jeff's friends as our own and spent the week doing what people in Placencia do when they aren't working — eating, drinking and hanging out with friends.

Jeff had recently won a snorkeling trip at a charity auction and invited me to tag along as his guest. Belize is a mecca of snorkeling and scuba diving, with an offshore barrier reef that stretches nearly 200 miles — the longest in the western hemisphere — along with a handful of atolls and hundreds of other islands dotting the waters between the reef and the mainland. Laughingbird Caye, the jumping off point for our snorkel tour, was the quintessential picture-perfect deserted island. We saw all manner of colorful fish, beautiful jellyfish, and even a sea turtle or two.

Over the weekend, we spent a day at a waterfall/swimming hole in the mountains, about 45 minutes outside Placencia. We traveled in typical Belizean fashion, in the back of a pickup, with new friends, expat and Belizean. The route took us through orange groves and banana plantations on a rough road with no signage. Since we were totally reliant on public transportation on our trip, even if we had known about the waterfall, there was no way we could have gotten there. We spent the day grilling food, cliff jumping, swimming and relaxing. It was a perfect day with great company and we were thrilled to feel included.

While in Placencia, we even attended the oceanfront wedding of two complete strangers who'd basically invited the whole town to celebrate with them. Jeff knew the couple, so we also joined in and watched as they were married on a dock by the ocean, each with a Belikin, the beer of Belize, in hand. We were grateful to Jeff and his community for welcoming us completely. Without our couchsurfing connection, there is no way we'd have been able to relax as fully or experience this place so deeply.

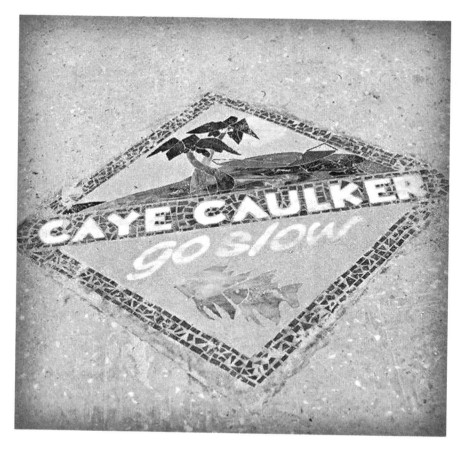

13. Caye Caulker, Belize (Days 63 to 71)

After four days in Placencia, we were ready to head on to Caye Caulker, our favorite spot from our first trip to Belize, so once again, we were heading somewhere familiar. Caye Caulker is a small enough island that there are no cars. Motorized transport is limited to golf carts, and none of the roads are paved. The town motto is embedded as a mosaic in the road and seen by every person who walks from the water taxi dock into town – "Go Slow". With a population of just 1,600, it is a quiet and colorful tropical haven and we love it. We were back on our own and content to wander.

We spent several days adhering to the town motto. We spent time swimming at the beach every day and started each morning with fry jacks stuffed with eggs from the shack down the street. Fry jacks are a popular Belizean breakfast food, made from flat triangles of dough that puff up when dropped in hot oil and can be stuffed with eggs, refried beans or breakfast meats. They are delicious!

We spent the majority of our time exploring the island on foot, something we hadn't had time to do on our previous trip. We didn't cover too much distance each day because it was so hot and humid that I found it difficult to go more than four hours between cold showers. Luckily Caye Caulker is the ultimate laid-back destination and since it's a tiny island, just four miles long and less than a mile wide, rushing wasn't really necessary.

On one of our walks we discovered a street sign that we couldn't help but love and that to my knowledge exists only in Caye Caulker. It depicts an airplane that looks like it has bounced off the roof of a golf cart. It seems to mean, "Caution, you are about to cross an active airport runway." There's nothing else in the way of warning, just a really cute sign. There are only a few flights a day, so you know, just a little heads up.

The economy on Caye Caulker is basically a combination of fishing and tourism, gradually shifting toward tourism. The fastest transportation available is arguably either golf cart or a bike and many of the businesses are so informal it looks like the owners just stuck a sign in the front yard of their homes. Even the local lumber store and fire station look like modified homes. The culture is exceedingly casual. A perfect example was a laminated sign showing a photo of a man dressed in a worn, white t-shirt and advertising his candidacy for a local office.

You get the feeling here that nothing is taken too seriously, even safety. Case in point were the electrical linemen. I don't know a whole lot about this job, but I know this isn't what it looks like back home.

As we wandered around the nooks and crannies of this small island, we stopped to watch fishermen catching small fish from the wooden docks, a variety of shore birds hunting in the mangrove swamps and hundreds of iguanas emerging from behind every rock and tree.

Once we left the main part of town, we were fascinated by the abundance of conch shells. There were piles of them everywhere. In some spots people had even cleverly built decorative walls with them. I knew that conch was a popular seasonal dish in coastal Belize, but I had never given much thought to what happens to all the rather large shells once their inhabitants have become dinner. Some more enterprising residents made all manner of jewelry and trinkets from the beautiful pink shells, and there were stands selling these items up and down the main street.

As much as we again enjoyed Caye Caulker itself, our hotel selections were not a highlight. One of our selections in fact, I feel I need to mention as it holds the distinction of worst hotel of our entire trip.

We had picked a place off the beach based on ratings and cost, even though it didn't have Wi-Fi. We had our own kitchen and bathroom, like a tiny apartment. It was clean and roomy with everything we could need, and it was cheap. Although it did have this strange painting of natives running from a UFO...or maybe they were celebrating...

Then it started getting dark and we noticed we had some really large bugs…which I quickly identified as really large cockroaches. Still I was fine with this; there were only a few, they only showed up after dark and they seemed to limit themselves to the floor. The first night when I got up in the middle of the night to use the bathroom, I took a flashlight and paid close attention to the floor and didn't see any roaches. After washing my hands at the sink, I stepped backward without looking and suddenly felt something large and solid under the arch of my bare foot. I carefully shifted my weight to lift my foot to see a three-inch roach scuttle off. Now, you might think that this would be grounds for "worst hotel" designation, but this place, we would likely book again. It is the hotel we "upgraded" to that was truly awful. You know it is bad when you wish you'd stayed with the cockroaches.

We decided we wanted to move to a hotel on the main street with a view of the ocean and a Wi-Fi connection. We did some research and settled on another inexpensive option.

Even with excellent ratings, we still exercised caution and followed common travel advice to look at the room before committing. The room we looked at was unremarkable, but acceptable so we booked it for the following night. When we actually came to occupy our reserved room the next day, there was a different room available, one that faced the ocean and was on a corner facing the ocean. We thought that having a window both on the ocean side and on the adjacent wall would give us better air circulation so we took it, sight unseen.

When we got to our new room we found it did have two nice windows. What it didn't have was a ceiling fan (like the room we'd looked at previously) just exposed wires where, presumably, a fan used to be. As the night went on, we found other things our room didn't have – a showerhead for instance. It had just a rusty pipe protruding from the wall. And that window that faced the ocean – it also overlooked the street, down which every night and every morning, drove the mosquito-spraying truck.

This truck was mounted with a spray nozzle that spewed a mix of mosquito-killing chemicals and diesel. This nozzle sat at the perfect height and angle so as to spray directly in our window. Twice a day we and all our belongings got fumigated. We tried our best to avoid being home at those times of day or to go running into the courtyard when we heard the truck approaching.

The room also had one of the most uncomfortable beds I've ever slept on. The mattress was some type of well-worn odd-feeling foam that I sunk into way too deeply and inexplicably just didn't want to touch. I'm not that picky - remember, this is coming from the woman who was ok with sharing a room with monster cockroaches. I was carrying a sleeping bag liner for just this type of situation and it now earned its space in my bag.

Alas, our cockroach room had already been rented and there was no going back. We checked. We just had to laugh, take some photos, write a blog post and mentally note a few lessons learned. I added "check shower" to my pre-rental checklist. Unfortunately, I haven't come up with a guideline that would have avoided the mosquito spraying.

A week later, we caught the Water Jets International water taxi to the town of San Pedro on Ambergris Caye, probably the most popular place to visit for American tourists to Belize. We'd found it a little resort-y and expensive for our tastes on our previous trip and skipped it this time, heading straight on to Chetumal, where we'd started our Belize/Guatemala circuit just over a month earlier. This two-and-a-half hour ride in an enclosed, large, very modern and very fast boat was a treat after our previous water taxi experiences. When the Water Jets taxi dropped us off, we were back in Mexico and therefore had to go through customs, which they take very seriously.

While we got off the boat, the crew was busy lining up all of our luggage single-file on the dock. Once all the passengers were off the boat, they had us all line up single-file as well and the border patrol officers ran up and down both lines with their dogs. The dogs didn't care about me, but my luggage on the other hand...I cringed a little every time they went down the line and singled out my bag for an aggressive pawing. It happened every time they brought the dog down the line and I was getting increasingly nervous.

First, I didn't want to get in trouble in another country. I'm a little paranoid about getting in even trouble in my own country and try my best to avoid breaking even minor rules. Second, although I didn't have anything really bad in my suitcase, I did have a few things I suspected maybe I shouldn't technically have, but didn't want to lose. I was carrying a year's worth of birth control pills, three months of malaria pills and a bottle of medicine I'd bought for motion sickness in Mexico (which was really a prescription Parkinson's drug). I had no prescriptions with me for any of these and most were no longer in their originally prescribed containers. I thought all of these were reasonably explainable,

143

but I wasn't sure my Spanish was going to be adequate for the task.

Eventually, one of the officers pulled my bag and a few others out of the lineup and had the owners of those bags step aside while they let everyone else go. They asked if I had any prescription drugs and had me unpack my bag. On this trip we learned that how a situation like this goes depends a little on how composed you are and a lot on the mood of the guy in charge. Luckily, the officer who ultimately pulled us aside was really nice, spoke decent English and chatted with us about Colorado, where he happened to have lived in the past. As I unpacked my bag, I aimed for the malaria meds knowing they'd be simple to explain and were also easily replaced. I explained what they were and that I thought those were probably the issue. I held my breath. He seemed satisfied. Breathing a big sigh of relief, I began throwing everything back in my bag as quickly as possible, while trying to remain outwardly calm. I was a bit afraid he might change his mind and wanted to move on as quickly as possible.

From there we took a cab to the bus station and headed north to Cancun, back on the cushy Mexican bus with A/C and movies. The first time we'd ridden this route several years back, the movies were loudly broadcast over the speakers, so you had no choice but to at least listen to them even if you didn't watch. This time, there were headphones so you could choose, which we appreciated. We passed the time watching Gnomio & Juliet, Eragon, and The Devil Wears Prada, all in Spanish.

Although we'd visited a few times and the beach was nice, Cancun wasn't really our scene with its hotel zone packed with all-inclusive resorts and overpriced restaurants. However, to give ourselves a cushion before our flights to South Africa, we'd booked two nights at a bed & breakfast in the old town area of the city rather than the hotel zone. We found this to be an altogether different and more authentic experience that we'd like to repeat.

That night, we followed our host's directions to a huge plaza called Las Palapas where hundreds of families wandered, enjoying live music, carnival type games and dozens of food vendors. This place was packed and happening. One of the things we'd grown to love about Mexican culture was the communal, outdoor nature of life and this was a great example. Families were strolling around and kids were cruising by in colorful electric mini-cars. This seemed like the place to be and the atmosphere was welcoming, family-friendly and festive. We felt completely at ease and there were so many foods to try, many we hadn't seen anywhere else, that it was overwhelming. We finally settled on a few items, the most memorable being a marquesita. This is a traditional Yucatan dessert where cheese and caramel sauce are rolled up in a wafflecone-like wrapper. Cheese and caramel may sound like an odd combination, but the result is pretty tasty. Apparently an ice cream seller in the 1930s was looking for something to sell to his customers in the winter and, voila, we have the marquesita.

The next afternoon, knowing that in two days we'd be in Africa and we had no idea what would or wouldn't be available, we also took some time to see a movie. Iron Man 3 was playing at a mall theatre nicer than any in our home town at the time. Luckily for English-speakers, pretty much the whole world watches American movies and most countries don't bother dubbing the movies into their own language. They just slap subtitles on them, so the soundtracks are still in English.

After our movie, we returned to the B&B and turned in early, hoping for a good night's sleep before heading off on a marathon of plane travel to reach South Africa. A whole new continent was waiting and we wanted to be ready, or as ready as possible.

14. South Africa – Arrival and Zulu Nyala Safari (Days 72 to 80)

Not surprisingly, there are no direct flights from Cancun to Richards Bay, South Africa, and since we were using earned airline miles to make the trip, the options were further limited. However, we figured if we were going to use miles for a free flight, this was the one. A long and infrequently traveled route between two continents is usually a better value than a straightforward jump between two hubs on the same two continents. At the time of this writing, a one-way ticket from Cancun to Richards Bay "cost" 45,000 miles but the flight would run at least $1,500. For comparison, the mileage award needed to fly from NYC to Johannesburg (still North America to Africa) is slightly lower at 40,000, but that flight would cost only $900. Using miles for less common routes and to/from smaller cities usually has the biggest payoff.

By this point in our trip, my parents were settled back on the East Coast and we'd been utilizing their address to ship and stockpile items we wished we'd thought to bring with us and had subsequently purchased online. We had booked our flight from Cancun to South Africa before heading out from Colorado, so we knew we'd be passing briefly through the U.S. with layovers in Washington, D.C. and New York. The layover in D.C. was 12 hours and we'd convinced my parents to make the three-hour drive to meet for dinner and to let us trade out gear, dropping what we didn't need and picking up our online purchases. They graciously agreed, even though the D.C. layover was less than ideally timed. We were scheduled to arrive at 8 p.m. and depart again at 8 a.m. – just enough time to navigate customs, catch up over a late dinner, grab a 5 a.m. hotel breakfast and shuttle back to Reagan International Airport. Luckily, our flight was on time.

It was fantastic to see my parents and we stayed up far too late chatting over dinner, unwrapping our new items and repacking our bags. We were all staying the night and sharing a room, so it was hard to stop talking and by the time we got to bed it was 1 or 2 a.m. We'd barely closed our eyes when the alarm went off at 4:30 letting us know it was time for a quick breakfast and a trip back to the airport. We said our goodbyes and set off for Africa.

As a quick summary of the travel marathon we were in the midst of, we had left Cancun at 4 p.m. on June 10. That night we were in Washington, D.C. with my parents, where we managed about three hours of sleep. The next day we passed through JFK with a one-hour layover and then made the 15-hour overnight flight to Johannesburg, on which we also got very little sleep. After a four-hour midday layover in Johannesburg, we caught a fourth flight to Richards Bay. This landed us in Richards Bay just over 41 hours after taking off from Cancun. There was a seven-hour time change, and we'd only slept about four hours.

Next, we picked up our rental car. We tried to wrap our brains around South African insurance details, which seemed far different from anything we'd ever encountered, and learned to drive a manual transmission on the wrong side of the road. Well, Daryle learned this last bit, while I sat in the passenger seat, on the wrong side of the car, and tried to keep my mouth shut. This next photo was not taken that day. In hindsight a cab to the hotel might have been an intelligent choice.

It was 4:30 p.m. in Richards Bay, but we were barely managing to function and, I cannot lie, the drive was scary. We had a map, but since we couldn't find a single street sign, it didn't help much. The roads were winding and I was sure we were going to be bringing back a car with the raking marks of tree limbs down the passenger side, as we seemed to be scarily too far on the left side of the road. After several U-turns and some backtracking, we found a large mall with some distinctive road features that we were able to match up with the map by shape and landmarks. By the time we got to the hotel and found something to eat, it was 7:30 p.m. In my 40 years, this is the most exhausted I recall ever being.

This is an appropriate point to take the opportunity to thank my husband for being the ever-present voice of reason and rationality. The actual planning of travel – looking for flights, booking hotels, finding the best deals, etc. – is something I love and in general am good at. However, I sometimes get overzealous trying to fit everything together like a perfect Tetris game and Daryle has to step in with his calm, well-reasoned opinion. This, bless him, was one such time.

When I was booking these reservations in an excited, well-rested state of mind back in Colorado, I had thought we'd land on the 12th and start our safari on the 13th; why waste time? Daryle had immediately questioned that decision, insisting that we needed to add a buffer to acclimate to the time change and deal with our likely jetlag before we'd be ready to start 6 a.m. daily safari drives. As an African safari is a once-in-a-lifetime kind of experience it would be a shame to sleep through it. Once suggested, this seemed like a very reasonable idea, particularly since we weren't on a tight timeline so I booked us two nights in Richards Bay before heading on to our safari lodge.

I have never been more glad to have listened to my husband's suggestion. We slept 16 hours that first night and still had to do everything in our power to pry ourselves out of bed the next morning at 11 a.m. I am pretty sure I could have slept soundly all day. However, we had a safari to prepare for and we were trying to get ourselves acclimated to the time change and ready for that 6 a.m. game drive. We forced ourselves out and visited a local mall in search of a converter for our electronics and a fleece jacket for Daryle (it was winter in South Africa, a welcome change from a brutally hot late spring in Central America). In hindsight, it would have been smart to purchase the converter at one of the several airports we'd passed through filled with travelers, rather than at a mall where most shoppers were locals

151

with little need for converters of this type. We did eventually find one, but it wasn't as easy as we would have liked.

At the mall, we enjoyed excellent lattes and breakfast at 3 p.m. When we had finished up with our food and indicated we were ready to pay the check, our server asked us, "Do I need to bring the credit card machine?" which earned him blank stares from both of us. My tired brain ran thru all kinds of scenarios of what he might mean, including rolling a mobile ATM out to our table.

Finally, after what seemed like five minutes, but was probably 15 seconds, we recovered and did what any sensible, confused human should do; we asked. It turns out he was simply talking about a cordless version of the countertop machines used at just about every retail store back home. We found that the idea of a credit card leaving its owner's sight was nearly unfathomable in most places we visited outside the U.S. Bringing the machine to the customer in a restaurant seemed like such an obvious fraud prevention measure that we wondered why it wasn't common practice in the States as well.

Another unexpected source of confusion we'd encountered since arriving in South Africa was car insurance, so I spent a significant amount of time researching auto insurance liability as well. The previous day, I'd been very confused about the insurance situation when picking up our rental car. We were familiar with the idea of a Collision Damage Waiver – additional coverage to protect the car itself from damage. Our credit card covered that, so we declined. What confused us was the seeming lack of an option for liability coverage. In the U.S. we would have needed a policy to cover damage to another car or injury to another person if we were at fault in an accident.

We determined pretty quickly that damage to property is simply the responsibility of the owner of that property, regardless of fault. This made sense and was not a completely foreign idea to us. What took more serious research and caused more of a struggle to wrap my brain around was how South Africa deals with bodily injury. After an hour on the internet, what I came to understand is that South Africa actually has a fuel tax that funds a Road Accident Fund, which covers injuries sustained in car accidents. So in effect, insurance is paid for at the gas pump.

While I hoped not to test out how well this system worked, at least now we knew why there was no liability insurance being offered. We were as covered as we were getting. With that quasi-peace-of-mind, we headed back to the hotel for another long night of much-appreciated sleep before a one-and-half hour drive north to the Zulu Nyala Game Lodge.

When we'd originally begun planning this trip, it seemed like a year was a long time and we'd be able to do everything we'd ever dreamed of travel-wise. As we actually started putting together a rough itinerary, it was impressed upon us just how huge the world is and alongside that massive scale, just how relatively short a year is. Realizing we weren't going to be able to go everywhere we wanted, at least not if we wanted to enjoy it, and not on our budget, we started to narrow our focus a bit. We started by each choosing our top priority. Daryle's was several weeks in London. Mine was an African safari.

Prior to our trip, I was the fundraising director of a local non-profit organization. One of our big events was in November and in the past we'd had an African safari in our live auction. I made sure we had it again for our 2012 event and gave my husband free rein to bid. This purchase was part vacation savings, part Christmas gift from my parents and part donation to charity as far as our budget was concerned (so it didn't count in our average $85/day budget). We actually got a great deal on it as well. Having to buy your own airfare was a drawback to some, but perfect for us, since our travel plans were less than conventional – arriving from Central America and then staying in Africa for three months.

Africa was my dream come true from the very first day of our safari – everything I was hoping for and more. The package offered us lodging on a private game reserve for five nights, all meals and two game drives a day. I was in heaven.

We didn't waste any time and hit the ground running, arriving in time to check in, stow our belongings in our room and head out pretty much immediately on an afternoon game drive. It didn't take long for us to come across our first cheetah perched in a tree like so many photos. The cheetah then jumped gracefully down and walked within a foot of our Land Cruiser, never once acting like it was even aware of our presence. We went on to see amazing animal after amazing animal: elephants, white rhino, cape buffalo, nyala, impalas, hippos, giraffes, zebras and warthogs.

On our second drive the following morning, yes, at 6 a.m., we even saw the elusive leopard. Of the large critters, leopards are the only ones that can come and go as they please from fenced reserves like Zulu Nyala. There are frequently trees placed next to the game fences and leopards are good tree climbers and jumpers. Because they come and go and because they are stealthy and quiet, they can be really tough to locate. Luckily, our guide, Manie, was so good at reading the signs of the bush that it was like the leopard had a homing beacon. We were driving along at a good clip in the Land Cruiser, when Manie held up his hand for quiet and hit the brakes. He'd heard a bird in the bush make an alert call. He pointed off to our left and said matter-of-factly, "There's a leopard over there." He turned the vehicle off the path and plowed ahead. Sure enough, we got a view of a leopard loping along and then disappearing into some underbrush. She hunkered down there and we were able to get a bit closer and watch her for a while before another Land Cruiser showed up to share the view.

Being in the first vehicle to locate an animal, particularly an animal that is notoriously hard to find, is always a good position to be in. The guides have radios and share info when they spot some of the more difficult-to-find critters, but being there first generally lets you see the animals in their more relaxed and out-in-the-open state. We backed off and headed on our way. We saw the same leopard again on the next few drives until she presumably headed on her way out of the reserve. The best word I can come up with to describe her was "majestic." I felt like

I was in the presence of something holy, she was that beautiful and obviously powerful.

We didn't realize how lucky we were on our first few game drives until later. In fact, on our first two drives we'd seen four of the Big 5 and since our reserve didn't have any lions living there (the 5th of the Big 5), that was as good as we could get.

The Big 5 is a term originally coined by game hunters to refer to the most difficult and dangerous animals in Africa to hunt. The term is now used by safari tour operators and people hunting these animals with their cameras instead. The Big 5 includes the lion, elephant, Cape buffalo, leopard and rhinoceros.

Heading back to breakfast that first morning, I was thinking, this trip, and this part in particular, was the best thing I've ever spent money on. It was proving to be worth every penny.

For the next five days, every morning at 6 a.m. and every evening before dinner we were in the Land Cruiser trolling the 4,500-acre reserve for the most amazing wildlife I'd ever seen. Most days we at least saw the family of three elephants that lived on the reserve, along with the cheetah family, several rhino and always zebra, nyalas and giraffe.

And warthogs – the delightfully funny-looking critters made popular by Pumba in The Lion King. Warthogs were everywhere.

In fact, one day as we pulled into the parking lot at the lodge after a game drive, I noticed that the ground under our rental car seemed to have been oddly hollowed out. Pointing this out to Manie, he told us that a warthog had made its burrow under our car. While I was worried about being able to back out our tiny car without falling into the huge trough, Manie pointed out the more important concern was to make sure there was no warthog present before approaching the car.

Yes, good point Manie. I guess that's why they don't let us just wander around out here without a guide. Unlike in most of our daily lives in the States, where we might run into a squirrel, raccoon or maybe even a fox, in Africa we were dealing with animals of more serious consequence.

Manie was the quintessential Dutch South African. A big, strapping, fearless, down-to-earth rugby player with an excellent sense of humor. This was a guy who brought home baby warthogs abandoned by their mom to raise in his home with his wife and son, like some people bring home abandoned kittens. He knew the bush inside and out and knew how to make sure guests had a great experience, seeing lots of wildlife close-up, but also knowing the boundaries of safety.

Along with the safety and enjoyment of his guests, he had a genuine primary concern for the health and well-being of the animals and an uncanny ability to read their body language. This genuine concern for the animals was apparent one day when we returned from a game drive with a different, I'd wager less experienced, ranger. We'd gotten a bit too close to an agitated elephant and had very nearly been charged. This was certainly an exciting game drive and one our whole vehicle was still chattering excitedly about on our next drive with Manie that evening. I could tell he was irritated by it.

At first, I naively thought maybe he was jealous to have had everyone have such a great time out exploring with someone else, but once he explained, his reaction made perfect sense. He was angry that the elephants had been unnecessarily stressed. These animals are "visited" day in and day out in their homes, so it's critical that they be respected and not subject to unnecessary stress. The ranger's job is to entertain the clients, yes, but the more important long-term job is to look out for the extended health and well-being of the animals.

There is a way to view the wildlife without interfering and that day, we'd interfered. I knew he was right to be angry and immediately felt a little guilty about the rush I'd gotten from "escaping unharmed" and the subsequent adrenaline-fueled chattering of our entire group. Game management is a whole field dedicated to maintaining a critical balance – making it possible for people to see these majestic animals in their natural habitat, so they can be more fully appreciated and more likely to be preserved, while simultaneously making sure the animals' quality of life is not being compromised.

The majority of modern safaris are technically called photo safaris, in contrast to safaris of the past, which were primarily hunting safaris. There's been an accompanying shift in game management toward conservation. Besides the inherent value of these creatures, forward-thinking people have realized that these animals are more valuable alive than as trophies hanging on someone's wall. While some hunting still occurs, most people now come armed with cameras, making them not just tourists pouring money into the local economy, but evangelists for the conservation and preservation of this land and these rare and unique species.

Since Manie had done such a fantastic job of finding us every possible animal in the first 24 hours of our trip, I had to expand my "want to see" list for the week and get a little more specific in some cases. I wanted to see not just a mama hippo floating in the water with her relatively tiny and adorable offspring asleep on her back, but a hippo out of the water, which was far less common to spot. And I wanted to see a cheetah run. We managed both.

One morning, we were parked watching the cheetah family – mom, dad and a young male – lying around in the sun near one of the game fences at the edge of the reserve. Suddenly they all perked up, looking up the fence-line and dropping into alert, stalking mode, flattening themselves to the ground with hind ends wiggling in anticipation and pent up springing energy. We quickly saw that two blesboks, a common medium-sized species of antelope, were ambling their way in our direction but on the far side of the fence.

I'm not sure if they were aware of the cats' presence or not, but they kept coming, slowly walking along the edge of the fence until they were almost even with the cheetahs. At this point a cat twitched and the blesboks went sprinting back the direction they'd come. The cats didn't hesitate and immediately gave chase. It was a short chase, probably only about five seconds and I suspect not one at top speed, but still impressively fast and graceful. I'm relatively certain the cheetahs were aware that catching the antelopes wasn't an actual possibility, but it's hard for any cat to resist a chase.

In addition to all the grace and power we witnessed, we unfortunately also saw the disheartening impact of humans on these largely rare species as one of our drives brought us past the carcass of a rhino killed by poachers, the body left to rot once its horn was hacked off. In many cases, we learned, the poachers don't even wait until the animal is dead. This opened a conversation that taught us a lot about the realities of poaching. Often game rangers like Manie are leading clients during the day and then lying in wait for poachers at night, not only protecting their livelihood but the valuable sustainable resources that are a huge part of the local economy. This isn't a lifestyle that goes easy on a family and it's not one without risk. The risks are actually huge; poachers are generally well-armed and not afraid to use those weapons. Any confrontation is likely to end in a gun fight.

Poaching is run by professionals – international organized crime syndicates who rely on desperate locals to do the dirty work. Those doing the poaching aren't making the big bucks, but those higher up are making millions. Manie had crazy stories about spending nights out in the bush staking out the reserve to catch poachers.

If you read the news in Africa it doesn't take long to read about a game ranger killed by poachers. Being a park ranger in Africa is, like many things we discovered, a wilder more intense version of a thing we were very familiar with. Manie shared that he frequently wears a bulletproof vest even on his drives to and from work. He's known as someone who fights against poaching, and apparently that isn't a terribly safe position to be in.

As awful as the death toll of animals directly killed by poachers is, what was even sadder to me were the secondary casualties caused by the loss of these animals. If a mother rhino is killed, her young will most often die as well, unless they find another female to take them in. The youngest rhinos have only hours to find nourishment and safety. In addition, the young frequently witness their mother's death and suffer emotional trauma as well as physical injury if they get in the poacher's way. Manie not only gave up sleep to put himself in harm's way to save these animals, but spent his non-safari-guiding, non-poacher-hunting, waking hours pursuing his dream of opening an orphanage for abandoned baby rhinos. Needless to say we were impressed by his commitment.

15. Endoneni Cheetah Project & Bayete Zulu Game Reserve, KwaZulu Natal, South Africa (Day 77)

Like an all-inclusive-type resort anywhere in the world, our safari lodge had additional experiences and tours available. When we had first arrived we'd been given the rundown – a game drive at a nearby reserve that did have lions; a game drive at a nearby national park that was much larger than the reserve where we were staying; a boat trip at a coastal UNESCO site with lots of hippos; and two of what were termed "animal interaction" trips. We had signed up for both of the interaction trips and two days into our safari we got the opportunity to visit some elephants and cats, large and small, up close.

Following our regularly scheduled early morning game drive and breakfast, we hopped in our rental car (after checking carefully for warthogs), carefully maneuvered around the trough and headed off to the Cheetah Interaction, where I was looking forward to petting a cheetah!

In addition to cheetahs, the Endoneni Cheetah Project housed several other wild cat species, including servals, caracals and African wild cats. The Project was an education and breeding center that took in former pets and orphaned kittens, while releasing "surplus" cats into the wild when they are ready. In their own words, they existed "to create wildlife awareness in the community and local schools." Now, it may not be immediately apparent why awareness of wildlife needs to be created in a place where lions, leopards, elephants and cheetahs seem to be around every corner. However, there are actually only about 9,000 cheetahs left in the wild and we found again and again as we traveled that the local experience of a place is far different from the tourist experience. Surprisingly, the chances are great that a majority of local people have never seen, much less interacted with, the local wildlife that tourists come great distances to see. If there has been interaction it may have been negative – a lion hauling off critical livestock for instance. It's very difficult for a person who has either no frame of reference or a purely adversarial experience with local wildlife to understand why conservation is important. As with so many things, education is the key to understanding, which is the key to creating positive change.

The Endoneni Cheetah Project may have had the local community and health of the ecosystem top-of-mind, but they certainly catered to the safari tourist. I imagine that is how they covered the bulk of their operating costs; it had to be an expensive endeavor. Feeding time was open to visitors and tours were offered where guests could actually enter a cage with the African wild cats and servals, and as the highlight, pet a cheetah.

I love all cats, however cheetahs I find particularly unnerving.
You know they have to know you are there, but they give
absolutely no indication that's the case, even when you are
standing right beside them. They continue to stare off into the
distance, past or away from you, like they are purposefully
avoiding acknowledging your presence. Looking everywhere but
at you, they seem more aloof than your average cat. The feeling
is akin to when you try to make eye contact with a stranger on
the street to ask them a question and they are obviously working
very hard to appear oblivious to your presence. This was the
only animal we encountered like this and it seemed universally
true of every cheetah we saw, whether out in the wild or in

167

captivity. This inclination made it relatively easy to avoid eye contact with the cheetah, as we'd been instructed. Sustained direct eye contact is seen as a confrontational or aggressive behavior by cats – not a message you want to be sending to a 100-pound cheetah.

They weren't totally oblivious though, just aloof. Someone in our group naively tried to snuggle the cheetah when moving in for a photo op. The tourist got in the cat's face, talking in that babyish voice like people tend to do with a puppy, kitten or human infant. The cheetah was now most certainly directing all of its attention toward the offending woman and it did not look amused. Our guide jumped in quickly to intervene, looking a bit shocked.

The cheetah interaction was, of course, the finale - our first-up close encounter was with the African wildcats, a species, or rather subspecies, of cat I was unfamiliar with. African wildcats have a wide distribution throughout the continent and are generally recognized as the ancestor of the domestic cat. They are about the same size as a domestic cat (5-15 pounds and 33-40 inches in length), but their legs are proportionally longer. They are striped lightly all over with more prominent stripes on their legs and tail. A purebred African wildcat will have a tail that ends with a black cap. They eat rodents, small reptiles, birds and frogs, just like your domestic kitty might if she's allowed outdoors. These felines aren't currently endangered, but it has recently come to the attention of researchers and biologists that they could become so. Since they are closely related to domestic cats they can interbreed and in areas near human habitation this is happening at high rates. This hybridization among wildcats and domestic and feral cats is a growing concern and the focus of recent research.

We were able to go into the enclosure with these wildcats and had the chance to watch up close as they snatched up entire antelope steaks and warily dug in while guarding their meal from others. It was interesting to watch an animal that looked so familiar, but acted so differently than we were accustomed to. A housecat look, but an all wildcat demeanor.

We were also allowed to enter an enclosure with a pair of hand-raised servals – after they were fed. Servals are tree climbers and were fed by tossing steaks up into the tree where they snatched them out of the air. Once they'd been fed, one came down and wandered around, giving each member of the group a good sniffing. While he ignored most people, he seemed to single out Daryle and another woman in our group for particular attention, proceeding to rub all over them in a manner very similar to the way our housecat rubs against our legs or the edge of the cabinets. The difference with the servals was the quantity of slobber left behind. By the time we moved on, the leg of Daryle's pants was drenched from knee to hip in cat saliva. Manie, who'd driven our group over for the tour, was in a fit of laughter.

As luck would have it, Endoneni also had some serval kittens onsite that we were allowed to hold. Yes, hold. It's important to be able to quickly identify a once-in-a-lifetime opportunity and take it. I was super nervous to pick him up, but I knew I only had a few minutes to either reach out and gently grab him by the scruff or get out of the way and let someone else have a chance. The kittens were probably about 15 pounds and the size of large housecats, but longer and leaner. I was mildly terrified, but knew I'd regret it forever if I let the opportunity pass, so I took a deep breath and scooped him up. I would never have guessed that a serval kitten would purr, but as I held him that's exactly what happened. I quickly decided that servals were my new favorite animal.

This is still one of my favorite photos and memories from the entire trip, not just because the experience was unexpected and literally breathtaking, but also because it was a lesson in jumping in to take opportunities, whether they are comfortable or not.

After waiting our turn to pet and have our photo taken with the promised cheetah, we returned to the lodge for lunch.

This was a day full of awe-inspiring experiences and that afternoon we made a trip to the Bayete Zulu Game Reserve where we got to meet elephants Rambo, Rachel and Jubulani. Rambo was a huge bull elephant who had been hand-reared by humans after being orphaned. Every day, he leads his family up to the lodge to greet the guests. No one forces him, he just shows up. The elephants each have keepers that stay with them 24 hours a day and the most amazing thing to me was that those keepers are unarmed. This is a reserve with lions, rhinos and other large dangerous animals, but the elephants have accepted their human keepers as family and would defend them if necessary, even against lions.

Once Rambo and his family arrived, we had the opportunity to approach him, touch his giant tusks and humongous ears and even feed him. This entailed Rambo standing with his head towering directly above me, and me reaching up with a fistful of feed pellets to place them directly on his tongue. Example #2 that day of not thinking too hard and just taking the opportunity. Yep, I stuck my arm into an elephant's mouth. The result, besides a bit of an adrenaline rush and an elephant getting a snack, was an arm encased in slimy elephant saliva from the elbow down.

After this, we had the opportunity to feed Rachel, the female elephant, from more of a distance. She was still very protective of Jubulani, her calf, and it wasn't safe to get too close. The tourist experience on any given day during these interactions is dictated by the animal's mood, and at their keeper's discretion. Hand-reared or not, these are wild animals, enormous and strong wild animals that need to be respected. We fed Rachel from the far side of a low wooden fence by placing food in the tip of her trunk, which she then pulled back and shoveled into her mouth. Jubulani remained at her side the entire time.

The experience of being in Africa and on safari was blissfully surreal. Every day was like a dream of sorts where bucket list items were checked off in rapid succession. This feeling persisted as long as we were on the continent. It was a three-month succession of overwhelmingly amazing moments. This was just day four.

In addition to the plethora of wildlife we were able to see, being on safari was just plain fun. For the most part we were with the same group of people all week and with the same guide. In the morning, after driving around looking for as many animals as we could find, Manie would navigate to a spot with a nice view and good visibility so no rhinos or elephants could sneak up on us.

Then, we'd get out and stretch our legs, while he set up his French press on the hood of the Land Cruiser and produced a bag of Starbucks coffee beans. He proudly told us these beans had been sent to him from the U.S. by a former guest and that as far as he knew they were the only Starbucks beans in all of South Africa. This was a source of great pride for Manie and we really enjoyed the morning coffee ritual.

On the evening drives, we'd do the same thing, stopping somewhere to watch the sun set over the African bush. One afternoon we received a phone call in our room letting us know that our guide was "planning a sundowner" for our evening drive. We said that sounded great and hung up, quickly realizing we had no idea what that meant. We figured there must be some action to be taken on our part or the phone call wouldn't have been necessary. A sundowner, it turns out, is a British term for an alcoholic beverage enjoyed in the evening after work. This was the first of many British customs and terms we'd encounter in South Africa – holdovers from the days when South Africa was a British colony.

We gave ourselves a few extra minutes on the way to the safari rendezvous point and stopped by the lodge bar. As we hoped, when we told the bartender in a somewhat hesitant and questioning manner that our guide was planning a sundowner, he knew just what we needed and happily handed us a few beers. The photo we took that evening with beers in hand in front of a peaceful sunset with the African bush stretching to the horizon, for me, sums up our African safari. More than any other, this picture encapsulates the way I most like to think of myself and reminds me of the way I most like to feel – pleasantly tired, but exhilarated after a long day full of exciting adventures.

Because a major marketing technique of this safari lodge group was working with travel agents in the U.S. to offer safari trips to non-profit groups for inclusion in gala auctions, the majority of our fellow guests were also American. Having been in the country only a few days, we didn't realize this would be the only time during our month in South Africa, or really, during our three months in Africa, that we would encounter a significant number of other Americans.

Our group was fantastic and we enjoyed sharing meals and game drives with them. We were a bit of an anomaly in the group, being the only members in our late 30s/early 40s and possibly the only ones pulling in less than six figures. Most were there with family and a number were not just doctors, but specialty surgeons. While ordinarily we might have felt out of place, we unexpectedly found ourselves the objects of curiosity and good-natured jealousy. Being three months into a year-long international adventure gave us our own distinction that made us intriguing and we felt at home in a group that would not have been our typical companions back home.

Because we were traveling slowly, our trip cost a fraction of what the rest of our group paid. Time and cost are almost always inversely proportional and we learned to work time in our favor. For example, we found all of our safari companions had either already been to Victoria Falls or would be headed there when their safari was over. However, while they had only two weeks in southern Africa, we had six, so without fail, they took the $400 flight from Johannesburg, while we took the $40 bus and $12 train. Mind you, these are not equivalent experiences and each has its pros and cons, which I'll talk more about when I get to the Victoria Falls chapter, but the time/money trade-off made the experience of seeing this wonder of the world accessible, even on our $85/day budget.

The main attraction at Zulu Nyala was of course the wildlife, but the lodge itself was beautiful and we enjoyed having lunch on the patio overlooking the reserve every day. It was winter, but nothing like the winter we were familiar with as Coloradoans. It was more similar to early fall or mid-spring in the Rocky Mountains – cold enough to require all the layers of clothing we'd packed for game drives at 6 a.m., but very pleasant t-shirt weather by noon. It never got warm enough for me to want to use the well-appointed pool outside our room, but the weather was ideal for seeing animals, which was our main purpose after all. There wasn't a drop of rain all week and the absence of foliage made spotting the animals a lot faster.

It was easy to forget when we were at the lodge that we were smack-dab in the middle of the reserve without any additional fencing. We were staying there along with the critters we'd come to see and though most kept their distance, it was possible to run into any of the animals at any time. We'd seen plenty of kudu, a type of large African antelope, around the lodge grounds and obviously there were warthogs about. One night, after dinner indoors, we noticed more people than usual out on the second-floor balcony overlooking the reserve. We went out to see what was going on. There was a small pond just below the balcony and in the darkness we could just make out all three elephants wallowing in the pond and eating everything they could lay their trunks on. We stood out on the balcony for the best part of an hour watching, and in the morning at breakfast we could see what a mess they'd made of the formerly tidy little pond. It seemed that keeping the lodge grounds in the pristine condition we'd witnessed was more work than I'd imagined.

16. St Lucia, KwaZulu Natal, South Africa (Days 81 to 83)

After five days of relaxing and touring the reserve at Zulu Nyala, it was time to head off on our own to explore South Africa!

We knew shifting from the comfortable structure of the tourist-focused lodge would be a little intimidating, but also welcome. Things were about to get less predictable. Luckily for us, although South Africa has 11 official languages, English is the language of most public conversation and of business, so at least the language barrier would be minimal.

English is spoken in a surprisingly large number of African countries, particularly in the south and east part of the continent. Perhaps if I had paid better attention in history class, I would have realized what prolific colonizers the British were in the late 18th and early 19th centuries and been less surprised. Throughout our time in Africa, we found ourselves constantly and somewhat unexpectedly, stumbling over British traditions and words.

So language was not an issue as far as clear communication, but what took some getting used to was that everyone around us could speak three or four languages, if not more. This resulted in endless incomprehensible side conversations. For instance, Manie was an Afrikaner (a South African descendent of Dutch settlers) and many of the other game rangers were Zulu (one of many native tribes of southern Africa). All spoke at least Zulu, Afrikaans and English. When they spoke to us it was in perfect English, but there were always conversations going on between the guides in either Zulu or Afrikaans, and I was constantly wondering what they were talking about.

I have repeatedly told Daryle that I am curious, not nosy, but I am forced to admit to a predilection for eavesdropping that is frustratingly thwarted by multilingual societies.

Our original plan in South Africa had been to drive along the coast to Cape Town and then take the train back to Johannesburg, where we could catch a bus into Zimbabwe. We quickly discovered there were a few problems with this plan, the largest of which was that the imagined ideal of a leisurely drive along the coast was far from realistic.

We envisioned a relaxed itinerary of short drives with ocean views and stop-offs in small towns. This fantasy world collided quickly with reality when I started plugging destinations into Google Maps. The entirety of the drive we were proposing was over 1,300 miles, a decent road-trip in any country, and we had allotted only two weeks to do it. We quickly realized we'd be doing a lot more driving than anticipated and that we'd be looking at a few seriously long driving days. We had no idea just how long those days would seem.

Starting off, we were in a pretty built-up part of the country, not that different from what we were used to at home. Apart from the dirt roads required to access our safari lodge, a good bit of the drive to and from our lodge had been on roads that resembled small American highways, with a few notable differences. The traffic included a large number of tractor-trailers hauling heavy loads of eucalyptus from the numerous plantations located in this part of the country to sawmills and pulp and paper processing facilities. Most of the N2, the main road we'd been using, in this part of the country was two lanes, one each way.

Although passing zones were rare, passing was common. Instead of the faster car using the oncoming lane to pass, the slower car would pull onto the shoulder without slowing down. If there was a good bit of traffic, the shoulder became a pretty constant "slow lane."

On a more fun note, we started to notice a few nomenclature differences. For instance, we noted that instead of the WIDE LOAD signs we were accustomed to, these eucalyptus-hauling vehicles displayed an ABNORMAL placard. I admit, the difference in terminology made the wide loads more exotic and therefore more fun. It took a while for me to stop giggling a little each time we passed a truck with one of these placards. On a side note, having never been to England, there were many terms and customs that we initially mistook as uniquely South African that were in actuality legacies of British colonial rule, including the "abnormal" loads and serving baked tomatoes and beans with eggs for breakfast.

Our first destination on this epic road trip was the tiny town of St. Lucia and the iSimangaliso Wetland Park in the northeast of the country near the Swaziland and Mozambique borders. St. Lucia itself is a town of just over 1,000 residents on the southern edge of Lake St. Lucia, the largest estuarine system in Africa and, when we visited, home to over 800 hippos and 1,200 crocodiles. Lake St. Lucia is just one part of the 820,000-acre iSimangaliso Wetland Park, South Africa's first UNESCO World Heritage Site, so designated in December 1999. Its name means "miracle and wonder" and was pretty appropriate.

It was possible to see all kinds of wildlife in this park, including leopards, black rhinos, several antelope species and 526 species of birds. It had a beautiful reef for snorkeling and diving and was a great place for whale watching and dolphin sighting. In the summer, its beaches served as both a nesting site for loggerhead and leatherback turtles and a spacious waterfront for sunbathing and swimming. Unfortunately, given our aggressive driving schedule, we were only able to stay one night in St. Lucia and we didn't have time to enjoy most of the fantastic opportunities or activities afforded by the area. Being in a hurry when you are traveling really stinks we observed, not for the last time.

We got to town in the afternoon and after checking into our guest house, we drove straight to the edge of town. Here the road dead-ended at a boardwalk through the wetlands to the beach where the river exited the estuary and poured into the ocean. We were on a mission to see some more hippos and maybe finally a crocodile.

The signs along the boardwalk were promising if a bit fear-inducing, warning of a trifecta of dangerous critters: hippos, crocodiles and sharks. We headed off on foot, thinking of how different a little afternoon stroll felt with the addition of some dangerous wildlife.

We got a nice look at some hippos wallowing in the shallow water and chomping away on some tasty vegetation. While taking some photos, we kept what we felt was a safe, conservative distance, although I'm not sure what expertise we were basing that measurement on. We'd learned during our safari time that hippos kill more people than any other animal in Africa, approximately 3,000 a year. You might have thought elephants, or lions were a more likely candidate for this honor, but no, it's the rotund, goofy-looking hippo. Lions are responsible for just 250 deaths a year by comparison. Hippos are semi-aquatic, spending up to 18 hours of each day in the water, and that's where they feel safest. Wallowing in a lake or river, that's their happy place. However, some of the tasty greenery they enjoy is on land, and they venture out in the evenings to feed. In the early morning they return to the lakes and estuaries they call home. Unfortunately, this is also a common time of day for people to be collecting water, bathing or washing laundry in these same bodies of water. Hippos are territorial and not to be trifled with when feeling threatened. A hippo will charge for its safe spot, taking out whatever or whoever is in its path. Humans are likely to be on the losing end of this conflict, hence the hippo's title as deadliest mammal in Africa. (Mosquitos take the title as far as most deadly animal.)

St. Lucia is known as a place where you are likely to see a hippo wandering down one of the main streets. There are signs that say, "Beware of hippos at night," all over the place and it's important to remain vigilant. Africa certainly keeps you on your toes.

We heard at least one account of a town resident who wasn't paying attention when he came out of his house to use the facilities in the middle of the night. He startled some hippos that had been grazing nearby in the yard and was trampled to death. We were immediately pleased to have chosen a guest house with an ensuite bathroom.

Arriving at the beach, we got our first real look at the Indian Ocean. Being winter, the ocean looked cold and intimidating. It was incredibly windy, creating huge crashing waves and sandblasting every inch of bare skin. Knee-high clouds of blowing sand created a crazy, high-velocity moving layer of sediment near the ground with a noise akin to hundreds of slithering snakes. I didn't realize at the time that this stretch of coast is known for snorkeling, swimming and sunbathing in the summer. You never would have guessed it when we were there. We did gather though that there were some worthwhile fish to be had based on the large number of fishermen (even in this weather) with huge, strong poles anchored in the sand. I did a little research and found that marlin and sailfish are common catches.

We headed back to our guest house after our first afternoon in the area, having seen quite a few hippos, but still not a single croc. We hadn't decided what to do with our one full day in St. Lucia, but after careful consideration, we decided to forgo the popular estuary boat cruise in favor of a drive farther up the coast, into the wetland park to Cape Vidal. This was a 20-mile drive with several overlooks and a few walking trails. To the west, this drive showcases miles of estuary and swamp forest, while to the east is the vast Indian Ocean. We saw beautiful rugged coastline, dozens of hippos wallowing in the shallow waters of the estuary and swamp forests, a handful of zebras and, we think, even a few rhinos in the distance. (Binoculars would be something we'd recommend bringing on a trip to Africa.) From one of the viewpoints overlooking the Indian Ocean we even watched a humpback whale resurface repeatedly as it purposefully swam from one side of the horizon to the other, presumably on its migration route north to Mozambique.

Upon reaching Cape Vidal, a beach access point and the turnaround point of our drive, we decided it was a perfect place to have lunch. Before we even got to the parking lot, I noticed a sign that said, "Beware monkeys are a problem." Hmm, I thought as I diligently looked around for monkeys as we approached the parking lot. I saw not a single monkey. We parked the car, Daryle headed to the restroom and I opened the hatchback to dig out lunch. I realized I'd forgotten the forks in the glove box and quickly went to retrieve them. I was gone less than five seconds, and yet when I returned to the rear of the car, it was just in time to see a monkey disappearing with a bag containing half our loaf of bread. It seemed he had run full speed across the wide open parking lot, snagging the bag without even slowing down and continued past me, mouth agape, out the other side of the lot and into some trees where dozens of his monkey friends chased after him and his newfound snack. Damn it! When Daryle returned I told him the story of where our lunch had gotten to and we determined to be more vigilant in our monkey surveillance.

Luckily, I'd separated the pre-sliced portion of our bread into its own bag when planning for lunch back at our guesthouse, so we still had half a loaf safely in reserve. We sliced new bread for sandwiches and gathered up the rest of our food. Spotting a bench on the beach a good distance from any trees, we decided that it would give us a decent-sized buffer zone from simian troublemakers. We could still see them eyeing us and our lunch from far above in the trees, so we made sure the food stayed between us on the bench, with eyes and a hand on it at all times. However, there was just this one time, when my mind wandered and I suddenly realized I'd let my guard down. My lapse in strict attention lasted at most three seconds and I immediately refocused on the lunch between us, just in time to see a monkey hand reach through from the back of the bench, snag the rest of the bread and head full speed for the woods. Again, we watched as a monkey ran off through the trees with a good portion of our lunch held triumphantly in one hand, with a line of other monkeys in pursuit. Despite serious vigilance, we had our lunch stolen, not once, but twice in one picnic. I will never again underestimate a primate and I'll take a monkey warning sign seriously, even if I don't see a single monkey. The sneaky bastards are there somewhere, just waiting. Monkeys are a problem – indeed they are.

17. St. Lucia, Durban, Port Shepstone, East London & Addo Elephant Park (Days 84 to 88)

I continued to curse the monkeys as we drove the two hours back to Richards Bay where we stopped for the night. The next morning, we headed south on a three-hour drive to Port Shepstone. This section of the drive had a beautiful, though distant, ocean view and a decent multi-lane divided highway. About halfway to Port Shepstone, we passed through Durban, the third-largest city in South Africa, known for tourism and surfing.

South Africa is a study in contrasts, and the cities are a stark example. Before heading into what was a thoroughly modern urban landscape, with high-rises, fancy hotels and yacht clubs, we first passed through a band of clearly impoverished townships that thousands of people call home. These shantytowns were made up of tiny dwellings cobbled together from plywood, corrugated metal and plastic sheeting, built on steep hillsides, nearly on top of one another. Sanitation and electricity are hit or miss, mostly miss I suspect.

I've seen this in movies and I've never doubted the reality, but seeing it with my own eyes was shocking. It was impossible for me, a middle-class American, to fathom what that life would be like. We have serious poverty in the U.S. that I don't want to minimize, but we don't have thousands of people living in incredibly close quarters in huts made essentially of trash, without running water, electricity or some type of sewer system. And you can't brush it off, saying, "Well, it is Africa, isn't it all poor?" because no, it's not all poor. There's abundance and poverty, just like everywhere. Our next stop, once we passed through the ring of shantytowns, was the Gateway Theatre of Shopping in Durban, where we chose from over 40 restaurants in a food court that rivaled any I've seen in the States. If we hadn't needed to get back on the road, we could also have enjoyed an arcade, bowling alley, IMAX theater, regular movie theater or The Wavehouse, which is the reason we stopped in the first place.

The Wavehouse was primarily a surf park, which featured, among other things, a double point-break standing barrel wave and hosts international competitions. I'd never seen a wave park and certainly not one at a shopping mall. Since it was a very short detour from the highway, it was something I decided I had to see. Unfortunately, being winter, the larger features were not active, but there was a smaller standing wave that was in use.

Just like in most places in the world, there are plenty of people with a lot of money in South Africa, and there are plenty of people with very little. South Africa consistently rates as one of the most unequal societies in the world.

The manifestation of this inequality that really struck me was the physical proximity of ridiculous wealth and destitute poverty. I have never seen so many concrete walls topped with broken glass or barbed wire in my life. Behind these ugly walls were beautiful houses with fancy cars, and I quickly started to understand why South Africa has issues with violent crime. I guess it's not surprising that a large population living in the shadow of wealth, struggling to get by, while having little hope of escaping that situation leads to conflict. The overthrow of apartheid certainly removed some barriers and opened up more paths and options for those who'd been oppressed, but race is still a highly charged issue, and resources are most definitely still skewed. With that said, although economic inequality has increased since the end of apartheid, it has also begun to deracialize. A silver lining maybe. Since 1994, the black middle class has grown 78% while the white middle class has grown just 15%. However, over that same period, the number of people living on less than $1 a day has doubled.

After watching a little girl learning to surf at The Wavehouse, we got back on the road and headed south to Port Shepstone where we stayed at a surfer's hostel called The Spot. There was a full moon rising over the ocean and a path to a perfect deserted beach. It was indeed "The Spot" and we enjoyed a beer and a nice stroll after a day on the road. The next morning, we were up and out at 9 a.m. for a long drive.

We'd talked with another guest the night before who'd made the drive we were about to undertake several times. He recommended getting up early and being on the road by 6. We don't really like getting up early if it's not absolutely necessary, and Google indicated it should be about a five-and-a-half-hour drive. We stubbornly stuck with our original 9 a.m. plan, feeling optimistic based on our experience so far. We hadn't yet realized how much Google maps didn't understand about Africa, and we still unfortunately hadn't learned that lesson about ignoring the advice of locals at our own peril.

We got off to a good start, but the N2 – the flat, well-maintained divided highway we'd been on almost since St. Lucia – was about to devolve into a hilly, two-lane free-for-all. There were large trucks hauling heavy loads, like sugar cane and concrete blocks, and there were construction zones where traffic was reduced to one lane for miles. We easily waited 20 to 30 minutes at each construction zone – and there were many – as the vehicles going the other way had their turn. Besides the sheer length of these one-lane sections, another difference we'd noticed about construction in South Africa in general was that nearly all work was done by hand. There was little heavy equipment. Instead of digging holes with a backhoe, there would be a team of six men with shovels. We were told at some point that this was an effort to curb high unemployment – I have no idea if that is true or if it's an effective technique, but I saw an incredible number of men shoveling gravel, digging wide trenches and doing all manner of jobs I'd only ever seen done using machinery.

In the midst one of these one-lane sections of roadway, we encountered an accident where a car had careened off the highway on an especially steep section and landed hundreds of feet below. We spent over an hour waiting while both lanes of traffic were stopped so they could attempt to haul the car back up with a winch.

In addition, there were dozens of towns along the mostly rural route where things came to a complete stop. While the highway traffic inched along bumper to bumper, people on foot with huge loads balanced on their heads wove their way between cars. Mini-buses and cars lined the road and squeezed their way into traffic at will. Some of the larger towns had traffic lights, but not many of them worked. Most were just dark, making their presence just plain depressing, reminders of good intentions gone awry.

Everywhere we'd been so far in South Africa was fairly diverse – Zulu, Afrikaner, English, Indian. Here, in the interior portion of the Eastern Cape province, it seemed we were the only light-skinned people for miles. Having spent most of my life in rural Pennsylvania and northern Colorado, this was not a feeling I was familiar with. I'm not proud to admit that I felt conspicuous and uncomfortable in my new position in the racial minority. I can't tell you if anyone around me was noticing or not because I was too busy being uncomfortable.

Along this stretch of road was the birthplace of Nelson Mandela (it's also now his final resting place, although he was still quite alive when we passed through). I'd read there was a Nelson Mandela Museum and contemplated stopping even though I knew we were way behind schedule by this point. I kept a lookout for signs for the museum, but never saw any. I was not really surprised. This didn't seem like an area frequented by a lot of foreign tourists in search of museums.

When we were about an hour outside the city of East London, the sun was setting and darkness was falling. The main trouble with driving in South Africa when it's dark is that it is completely dark. There were no street lights and you'll recall that I mentioned the shoulder on a two-lane highway being regularly used as a lane of traffic for slower-moving vehicles. Well, it's also regularly used by pedestrians. You see the problem. More often than not, pedestrians were dark-skinned, dark-clothed and virtually invisible.

There weren't a lot of options available to us. Traveling slowly required us to use the shoulder, but if we traveled too slowly we were at risk of being hit from behind. Traveling at high speed down a dark and unfamiliar road carried its own risks. There was nothing around and nowhere to stop. We knew we had to keep going and made a serious mental note not to casually blow off the advice of an experienced fellow traveler so quickly in the future. We stuck to the shoulder and prayed we didn't hit anyone.

The drive took nine hours, and the last hour was nerve-wracking. By the time we got to East London we were at a low point for the trip so far. We still had to navigate several miles past town on dirt roads through fields and forest. Daryle was seriously questioning my remote lodging choice at this point and I couldn't blame him. When we finally got to the gate where we had to use our crummy cell phone to make a call to be let in, we were both supremely grumpy, frazzled and absolutely exhausted.

We parked our car, forced smiles and did our best to put on a good face to greet the owners of the guesthouse as we walked up the front steps. Miraculously though, the grumpiness and the tension began to melt away almost instantly. I have never been so happy to be anywhere as I was to be there. The Santa Paloma Guest Farm was peaceful beyond comprehension from the moment we got out of the car, and we instantly knew we wouldn't want to leave, possibly ever, but most certainly not in the morning.

We had reservations up the road a piece the next night and there was absolutely no way we could imagine heading back out on the road in 12 hours. We arranged to have dinner and spent some time talking with our hosts about the history of the lodge and also about our plans. It turned out the owner at Santa Paloma knew the owner of our next night's accommodations and was willing to make a phone call to see if our reservation could be pushed back a day. It could, and we gratefully went to sleep that night knowing we had a 36-hour reprieve.

We didn't get to bed right away though; first we spent much of the evening in front of a roaring fire in the living room joined by members of the family, human and feline. The owners had extended family in town staying on the farm and we were the only non-family guests. Far from feeling awkward, we were treated like family as well, only adding to the feeling of safety and sanctuary. This was the opposite of what we'd experienced all day, and we were incredibly grateful. Daryle decided my choice of lodging wasn't so bad after all.

In addition to being welcomed like family, we had the opportunity to meet a lot of fascinating people. We spent the most time with Alicia and her five-year-old son Finn, who spoke five languages. While he knew words in all five languages, he didn't have them all compartmentalized yet, nor did he realize that everyone didn't speak them all. It was always fun to see what language his next burst would come out in. We never failed to be amazed at how the people we encountered abroad tended to be almost universally bi-, tri-, or even quadrilingual. We quickly began to feel woefully inadequate with a grasp of only 1.5 languages between us. Luckily our one fluent language is versatile and spoken at least to some degree in most of the places we visited.

We started the next day with breakfast on the porch, where we could watch the zebras and horses that lived on the farm, followed by a short hike in the woods and general relaxing. I contentedly ended another day in front of the fire with a kitty on my lap, a full belly and a grateful spirit.

Although I wouldn't say we wanted to leave, we were rejuvenated and the next morning we were as ready to go as we were likely to get. Alicia had written down my email, promising to contact her husband, who was home alone at their house in Cape Town, and very probably a bit lonely with his wife and son out of town. She thought he might be amenable to a few guests. We didn't hold our breath but it was certainly a nice gesture.

We headed up the road to Addo Elephant Park and the Aardvark Guest House, which just happened to be next door to one of the most highly rated restaurants in the Eastern Cape, according to our trusty friend TripAdvisor. We went by the elephant park to explore our game drive options and decided on self-drive the following day, then we headed to Hazel's Organic Restaurant for a beer. We really enjoyed chatting with Randy and Hazel, the owners, and decided to come back for dinner the next night.

Unfortunately, the next day's weather was less than cooperative, raining hard all day long. You might think this would be just an inconvenience to the tourists, but it actually means your chances of seeing elephants is rather low. Although it's not like they have a cave to hide out in during foul weather, they seem to stay deep in the brush and aren't likely to be seen out and about. Disappointedly, we skipped the elephant park and tried to visit the reptile and raptor center nearby for something to do, but found it was also closed due to the rain and flooding. Instead, sadly, we spent much of the day in our little roundhouse doing onward travel planning and writing. No elephants for us. Once again, being in a hurry stinks and I don't recommend it.

We did, however, go back to Hazel's as planned for dinner and had one of the best meals of our trip. We got to enjoy a homemade, locally-sourced South African meal. I had a blesbok steak that was unbelievably delicious. (Remember the blesbok we saw back on safari? Turns out cheetahs know their tasty antelope.) We were sad not to be able to stay another day to make a second attempt at seeing some elephants, but unfortunately we still had a lot of miles to cover and we now knew that leaving late was a very bad plan.

18. Storms River Mouth, Plettenberg Bay & Robberg Marine/Nature Reserve, Western Cape (Days 89 to 90)

The next day we entered the Western Cape, the province that houses Cape Town, and what seemed to be the one most geared for tourists. As we drove, the hills began growing and the forests started becoming more predominant. In this region, the "Garden Route" is the most popular attraction. Not a specific "route" per se, it's more of an area – one that encompasses a collection of beautiful national parks, magnificent coastlines and artsy towns, with the N2 (the road we'd been following since St. Lucia) running through the center. Only staying on the N2 though, you'd miss a lot, so the key is to have time to take the side roads and explore.

This section of the drive was more what we were picturing when we envisioned our entire South African road trip. This is where we really started to fall in love with South Africa. While we're not at all sorry for all we did experience on our road trip, if we were choosing again with the same time constraints, we'd probably choose to start in Cape Town and take a loop drive from there giving us more time to explore this area.

Just across the border into the Western Cape, we took advantage of one of the beautiful national parks and stopped off at Storms River Mouth Rest Camp in the Tsitsikamma National Park to stretch our legs. Here the Storms River flows out to the Indian Ocean through a deeply carved, rocky ravine. From the rest camp we followed the attractively named Dolphin hiking trail along the rocky shore past small waterfalls and hidden beaches. When we finally got to the mouth of the river, we found it was traversed by a series of suspension bridges, two shorter bridges which carry hikers over an especially rocky section of coast and a third bridge which crosses the actual river's mouth. At 250 feet in length, this is a significant bridge.

We had only planned to go as far as the bridges, but as frequently happens with us, we went just a bit farther after being intrigued by a sign with an arrow that read "Lookout Point." Curiosity won out at this point, as it usually does, and we continued to follow the trail as it climbed, and climbed, and climbed, until we topped out with a view of the ocean crashing at the base of steep cliffs on one side and a misty view of the Tsitsikamma Mountains across a forested plateau in the other direction. It was a bit more of a hike than we'd bargained for, but was completely worth it.

We were finding South Africa to be an amazing and beautiful country with a surprise around every corner. South Africa has such incredible variety in wildlife, culture and landscape that we sometimes found it a stretch to believe that the place where we were yesterday and the place where we were today were in the same country.

Arriving back at the parking lot after our hike, we noticed a patch of towering bushes with leaves a little like oversized aloe and tall orange flower stalks that added another foot or two in height. Upon closer inspection, the bushes were crawling with dozens of guinea-pig-like rodents perched up to 5 and 6 feet high, balanced on the leaves and stretching out to eat from the flower stalks. A little research revealed they were Rock Hyrax or Rock Badgers, and a bit more research revealed the surprising tidbit that they are thought to be the closest living relative to the African elephant. What?! These little guys?! Like I said, South Africa is full of surprises.

We continued on to Plettenburg Bay where we stayed at another
in a series of amazing and surprisingly affordable guesthouses.
These comfortable accommodations invariably had hospitable
hosts, tasty English breakfasts and convenient locations.

Plettenberg Bay, or Plett as it was called by the locals, was a pleasant beach town and our base for another natural area hike. It was starting to be obvious we were in a more well-to-do part of the country with more tourism. This town of 29,000 offered a plethora of activities, including ocean wildlife trips, canopy tours and zip-lines, horseback riding and game drives. It also contained an array of touristy shops, including a stationary store where Daryle and I both indulged ourselves with new notebooks and pens. The joy I felt with my new purchase was immense and completely out of proportion with its source, but traveling as lightly as we were, I hadn't bought much besides food and tickets for transport in months, and really, what is better than a new pen!

Plett was also the home of my favorite roundabout of the trip. When I say favorite, I mean the roundabout that brought me the most amusement.

We were getting used to seeing roundabouts, used much more frequently in other parts of the world than in the U.S., particularly in countries with an English colonial past, which was turning out to be far more countries than I'd realized.

By the time we returned home from this journey, I'd seen a full complement of roundabouts from the insane 12-road convergence at the Arc de Triomphe in Paris to my favorite tiny roundabout-like suggestion here in Plett.

The roundabout in Plett was more of an intersection with an obstacle. There was a slightly raised circle painted with red & white stripes – about 10 feet in diameter – in the middle of the intersection with a 10-foot-tall statue of a dolphin in the center of that circle. In order to avoid a collision with the statue while flying through the intersection most drivers simply made a quick jog to the left.

Because it was "technically" a roundabout, only yielding, not stopping, was required of drivers in all directions and, if anything, it seemed people sped up as they went through the intersection. I was reminded of the Escaramuza event we went to back in Mexico, where the riders would navigate their horses on intersecting paths at high speeds with the goal of narrowly missing each other. That's what it felt like each time we went through this "roundabout."

Courtesy of Google Street View, here it is. I love the dolphin statue, but really, doesn't that just make it worse – adding admiring the statue to the list of options for the driver?

Hoping to get us out of the car for another good walk, I'd picked Plettenburg Bay as a place to stay so we could visit Robberg Nature Preserve, which I'd read had a well-rated 6-mile hike that featured a large seal colony. In addition to protecting a pristine peninsula jutting out into the ocean, the protected area extended out into the ocean as a marine preserve as well. The hike itself will likely remain one of my favorites for a lifetime. The terrain of the hike ranged from walking along open sandy beach to narrow trails along clifftops to boardwalks below towering cliffs. There was even a separate rocky island connected only by a band of sand whose width varied with the tide.

The route first followed the northern ridge, passing just below the Cape Seal lighthouse, the highest on the South African coast. Looking out on the calm bay from high above, we saw a pod of dolphins, and as advertised, hundreds if not thousands of Cape fur seals basking on shore and swimming lazily in calm pools. I read that it's not uncommon to also see great white sharks trolling the waters from the high vistas available along the trail, although they were notably absent on our visit. They apparently find such a large population of seals rather irresistible. There are also three species of dolphins and five types of whales that frequent these waters throughout the year.

The return trip could not have been more different, following the rocky southern coast. This part of the walk was at and just above sea level. The ocean on this side of the peninsula was rough and forbidding. We saw dozens of seals here too, floating, surfing and jumping in the huge waves. For such a relatively short hike, the variety of landscapes was amazing, and seeing seals, dolphins and even whales off in the distance made the experience nearly perfect. We'd been doing a lot of driving the last week and it was really nice to be out moving about in the sunshine.

The weather had been gorgeous, and winter in South Africa was turning out to be rather comfortable. It was a lot like spring in Colorado, with 60°F to 70°F highs, and lows around 40°F at night. Interestingly, we found that very few places had central heat and the tendency was to open up the houses during the day for fresh air. We'd been thankful that our last guesthouse had a space heater and this one had an electric blanket. I had thought it seemed a little overconfident to me to not even install heating, but sometime around this point in the trip, we realized that the wall-mounted A/C units that nearly every house had, also served as fairly decent heaters. While not as heavy-duty as the heaters we were used to, they were likely adequate for winter here. Our guest rooms were considerably more comfortable from this point on.

19. Knysna, the Southern Tip of Africa & Hermanus, Western Cape, South Africa (Days 91 to 94)

Since leaving Santa Paloma, we'd been on a slightly more relaxed driving schedule. Thankfully there'd been no more after-dark arrivals and we'd had additional full-day layovers in Addo and also Plettenberg Bay. We'd only been booking guesthouses a day or two in advance to keep things relatively flexible, and after our day spent hiking at Robberg, we were starting to feel recovered from our marathon day behind the wheel. However, our rental car was due back in Cape Town in five days and we had a commitment in Kenya in three weeks, so we were starting to run low on time.

From Plett on, we moved into a slightly more hectic travel schedule. For the next five days each drive was supposed to be three hours or less, but there would be no more layover days. Despite each town having a lot to see and experience (it seemed like towns were getting more appealing and more packed with potential activities each day), we went straight from place to place, packing up each morning, unpacking each afternoon. With less than 24 hours in each place, we did the best we could. We were now only 400 miles out of Cape Town and visiting areas increasingly popular with tourists.

Our next stop was in Knysna, maybe one of the best known, most visited of the Garden Route towns. It was a pricier town and we were fortunate enough to land Couchsurfing accommodations with an amazing couple on a property a bit out of town. Etienne and Julie were in the process of converting their property to a guesthouse and nature reserve, and they were wonderful hosts.

They took us to see the Knysna heads (two giant sea cliffs that mark the entrance to and protect the lagoon that the town of Knysna is situated on), to dinner at a nice pub, and to our first microbrewery since leaving Colorado. Back at their house they showed us around and introduced us to their chickens, guinea pigs, ducks, dog and cat. The only problem with our stay was that we had to go so soon; we would like to have stayed for a week!

The next morning we were up early and headed three hours down the road to Swellendam, where we stayed at yet another beautiful guest house. It rained that afternoon and we spent our little bit of time walking around town in the rain trying to figure out where to eat…not really a very exciting day. There was a small farm on the way out of town advertising fruit and wine tasting that sounded nice, but not in the rain or at the beginning of a day's drive. Once again, we lamented being in a hurry.

The next day we headed for the town of Struisbaai and Cape Agulhas, the southernmost tip of Africa. We took a detour, aka the long route, on dirt roads because I'd read about De Hoop Nature Reserve as a great place for a hike. It turns out I was being overly optimistic about time and what we could fit in. The weather was less than ideal and we barely had time to get out of the car once we got there, never mind go for a hike. I'm sure in better weather with more time it would indeed have been a delightful hike along the sea as I'd read in guidebooks, but all we really accomplished was a longer drive than necessary. I sometimes have an issue confusing what can be fit in a day with what can be enjoyed in a day. This was a rather unsatisfying day because it was too much of the former and not enough of the latter, and we'd traded time on the road for time available at our destination without any payoff. Daryle was staying quiet about it – a bit too quiet perhaps.

There was a memorable moment on the road though, when something up ahead caught our eye. As we got closer, we realized there were sheep pouring down the hill toward us. It quickly became apparent that we had no option but to put the car in park right where we sat and watch as we were engulfed by a sea of baaing sheep. As they flowed around the car, we noticed that all were obediently veering to the right at the last moment and staying on the road, except one fellow whom we could see hesitate as he approached our car. We saw him look left, then look tentatively around at his compatriots going right and then he made a quick break to the left on his own. His rogue journey was short-lived as he merged with the herd once he'd passed our car. Sheep aren't known for their daring, but as the last sheep approached we could see a few shepherds frantically running through nearby fields directing a handful of disobedient stragglers back to the herd.

Being stopped to watch this unexpected parade of livestock brought me joy and amusement and thankfully eased the tension that had built between Daryle and me. It got me out of my head where I'd been worried about "wasting a day" instead of just living it. Daryle and I laughed out loud as we watched, and somehow the interminable drive was suddenly and unexpectedly redeemed. An otherwise unremarkable and dreary day became a day we'll always remember with a smile.

This experience reminded me how important it is to stay open and not to write something off that isn't over yet. A memorable moment can strike at any time and its critical to be able to recognize and embrace it when it does.

Between the sheep and the dirt roads, this drive turned out to be longer than the planned three hours, closer to four or five, and we were tired when we finally got to our hostel in Struisbaai. No rest for the weary, at least not today. Noting that we still had several hours left before sunset and no rain actively falling from the sky, we dropped our bags at the hostel and immediately hopped back in the car to head down the road to Cape Agulhas, the southernmost tip of Africa.

When we got to the parking lot, there were only one or two other cars there. We followed the sign pointing to the "Southern Tip of Africa," down a deserted boardwalk along the shore, until we reached a stone monument. Picturing the southernmost tip of the African continent on the map and knowing I was really standing there, over 9,000 miles from home, was surreal. I think what made it so unbelievable in part was that it felt not so much exotic and foreign as I would have imagined, but tame and familiar.

We used our camera timer to take our photo in front of the monument, and then I decided I wanted a photo of us sitting on top of the monument, which proved to be a bit more difficult than imagined. The monument top was chest height and I figured with a running start we'd be able to make it. I may not have factored in that I am not quite as young as I once was. We captured a collection of comical shots where one of us made it before the shutter clicked but not the other – one where Daryle rolled an ankle trying to use a pile of rocks as a step, one where I slammed into the concrete pillar with such force I thought I'd re-injured the rib I'd broken surfing in Mexico, and one where I was laughing too hard to make the jump at all. At this point, a family wandered by and took pity. Having witnessed the last few of our failed attempts, they offered to take the photo for us. That is the photo you see on the right.

This was one of those moments where you can't help but think to yourself – am I really here? Is this really happening? I'm really at the southern tip of Africa!!

We used every bit of daylight to explore the small town of Struisbaai before heading back to the hostel. We took a walk on the boardwalk and beach, finding dozens of dried-out wild sea sponges washed up on shore – the kind you pay good money for at a fancy bath & body shop. We made the most of our afternoon here, but again really wished we had more time.

We still needed to eat dinner, so we found a pub near the hostel. It had been a while since we'd had pizza – my hands down favorite food, so I was eyeing the pizza section of the menu and noticed bananas were a topping choice. Hmmm I thought, since I'm going with a totally familiar food, why not try a little twist? Pineapple is my favorite pizza topping, why not bananas? It turns out bananas on pizza are absolutely delicious. Particularly with garlic and bacon. I highly recommend it.

Being off-season, the hostel was relatively quiet when we returned for the evening, which suited us perfectly well and we spent several hours chatting in the hostel bar with Hector, a hotel owner from Spain; Erin, the South African part-owner and bartender; and a number of her friends from town who'd come by to hang out. We played a game called 30 Seconds, which was a sort of $25,000 Pyramid-like game, where you tried to get your teammates to guess as many names on your card as possible in, you guessed it, 30 seconds. Being a South African game, the names were mostly South African people, places and things, which put us at a distinct disadvantage competitively, but made the whole experience far more fun and memorable. There were also several rounds of a drink that Hector couldn't believe we hadn't tried and that he kept ordering for us. Unsurprisingly I can't remember the name of the drink, what was in it or how many I had.

Hector also shared his philosophy on when bad things happen while you are traveling. He told us, that he believes this is precisely when you know things are about to get interesting. He followed this with an illustration. Sometime ago he'd been on a solo motorcycle trip when his wallet was stolen. This led to adventures with a great group of people who'd come to his rescue that he never would have met had things gone as planned. As someone who has now spent a considerable amount of time on the road, I have to say Hector's theory rings true. Misfortune, or at least the unexpected hiccup, is often the beginning of the most magical, serendipitous experiences on the road.

In the morning, we headed off to the town of Hermanus, a brief hour and a half up the coast. Hermanus' full name was originally Hermanuspietersfontein. The postal service apparently found this name a bit cumbersome and shortened it. I had noticed a predilection for long names here. Afrikaans seemed to be like German in that you can keep adding to a word to give it a more specific or descriptive meaning.

Hermanus is known for its whale watching. In fact, you can see Southern right whales from the cliffs near the town center. No need to leave terra firma. We were lucky enough to be there during the winter, which is whale-watching season and as I mentioned earlier, not really all that wintry.

Two Whales!

We spent our few free hours in Hermanus walking along the paved paths that criss-crossed the cliffs and were satisfied to spot several whales bobbing not all that far from shore. I've been lucky enough to see whales on several occasions, but never from land, and somehow it felt different, like they were visiting our world instead of the other way around.

It's worth mentioning that there is another popular activity in this area that is a bit less relaxing and more adrenaline-inducing. Had we had more time to explore, there were no less than four different tour companies willing to take us cage-diving with great white sharks, but as we were running short on time we had to pass on that opportunity. Perhaps next time...

20. Arrival in Cape Town & Hout Bay, Western Cape, South Africa (Days 95 to 98)

The next day we drove another hour and a half and finally arrived in Cape Town, South Africa's second-largest city and the end of our epic road trip. We returned the rental car without incident and explored the Victoria & Alfred Waterfront area (V & A Waterfront) while waiting for Maarten, our Couchsurfing host, to get off work and pick us up on his way home. We suddenly found ourselves in a thriving, modern and sizeable city. It would have been easy for us to forget we were at the southern end of the African continent. With a population of just under one million,

Cape Town has all the amenities and the feel of a modern European city, including the obligatory Ferris wheel-type installation – the Cape Wheel at the V & A Waterfront.

Because we were schlepping luggage, we were prevented from exploring too broadly, but at least we could enjoy the beautiful weather and do some people watching.

The V & A Waterfront is named after Queen Victoria and Prince Alfred, her second son, who began construction on the harbor in the 1860s. It's South Africa's oldest working harbor, but also a hub of shopping, eating, entertainment and luxury living. In addition, it's the jumping-off point for touring Robben Island, where Nelson Mandela spent 18 of his 27 years in prison.

Visiting Table Mountain was on the top of our list of things to do while in Cape Town, so the following morning when the weather looked promisingly clear, we hopped on the bus to town to attempt to get a view from the summit. No matter where in the city you are, Table Mountain dominates the landscape and serves as a good landmark and compass for getting around. The mountain is really a two-mile wide plateau, 3,563 feet at its highest point. Considering that most of the city is at sea level, this is a sizeable monolith, edged with steep, impressive cliffs. Even at its lower elevations the grade is incredibly steep.

Unfortunately, it's pretty common even on otherwise clear sunny days, like this one, for the mountain to remain draped in clouds all day long – so common in fact that the cloud itself has a name. It's known as "the tablecloth." We spent the day at the waterfront again keeping a constant eye on the mountain and its cloud, ready to make a break for it if the clouds cleared. They never did, but we took this opportunity to try out something called bunny chow, a food that had caught my eye because of its unique name when investigating South Africa online.

Absolutely no bunnies were harmed in the making of my bunny chow. This South African fast food dish was made from a loaf of bread, hollowed out and stuffed with meat and vegetable curry.

The dish originated in Durban, which has a particularly large Indian community, and although it's not certain, it's likely that this meal was created as an easy takeaway (or take-out depending on where you are from) during apartheid, when Indians weren't allowed in many establishments. It's now on most lists of must-try street foods of the world. The best part of the dish in my opinion was the curry-soaked walls of the bread bowl.

Hout Bay, where our Couchsurfing host lived, had a population of 42,000 and was just far enough from Cape Town to be considered a separate town rather than a suburb. Located on a picturesque bay on the west side of the Cape Peninsula, it was a beautiful place to visit in its own right. We spent two days exploring – one alone locally on foot and one with our host Maarten chauffeuring us around the peninsula as tour guide.

On day 1 we found The Market, a weekend market held in an old fish factory on the working harbor with crafts, music and food. We'd heard there were often seals to be sighted in the harbor and I'd gotten my hopes up. The seals did not disappoint. I'm not used to having seals as local wildlife, so it was interesting to see them not just swimming off at a distance but interacting with a few local dogs who weren't so happy with their presence. One dog was more hesitant staying on shore, but the other would wade out into the water barking toward the submerged seal only to have the seal surface and bark back, which caused the dog to beat a hasty retreat. This was rather entertaining and went on for some time.

After we'd been watching the seals for 15 minutes or so, a young boy arrived with a pail in hand. I imagine he saw the small crowd gathering and sensed opportunity. It turned out he'd trained several of the seals, particularly a very large one (I would venture to say one of the fatter seals on the planet), to jump for fish held in his hand and even to take fish held gently between his teeth. Sea World trainers had nothing on this kid. He'd take a small fish from his bucket, place it between his teeth and lean out over the water. The seal would jump up to take the fish and the boy would take a bow and ask for money from the crowd. It was a new variation on street performance.

On day 2, Maarten had the day off from work and had been looking forward to showing us the Cape Peninsula. This was yet another experience made possible by Couchsurfing. The only way to really see the sights on the peninsula was with a car, and after the drive from St. Lucia, our car rental budget was exhausted. Not only did we get the transport, we got a local guide. We started our day-long private tour of the peninsula at the South African Naval Museum in Simon's Town, followed by something that had been on my bucket list for some time.

Boulders Beach is well-known, within South Africa and beyond, even appearing in several South African Airways ads in internationally-distributed travel magazines. Not only is this a particularly gorgeous coastal area where hundreds of huge 540-million-year-old granite boulders poke out of the ocean, forming protected rock pools and small bits of sand, but this beach is home to a breeding colony of 2,000 endangered African penguins. The opportunity to see penguins in the wild was something I'd dreamt about, and to have that opportunity without having to go anywhere extremely cold or remote was even better. The beach was every bit as beautiful as in the ads, and there were indeed hundreds of penguins visible.

One thing the photos don't share with you, however, is the smell of 2,000 penguins...pungent and overwhelmingly potent. If you've been to the penguin house at any zoo, you have a hint of what I mean.

Leaving Boulders Beach, we saw another of my favorite signs.

After the penguins, we had a visit to Cape Point, a nature reserve and World Heritage Site with trails that led to a lighthouse perched high above the ocean with panoramic vistas.

The tip of the Cape Peninsula is also known as the Cape of Good Hope and was once thought to be the dividing point for the Atlantic and Indian oceans. Although it feels and looks like you are standing at the tip of the African continent here, with the benefit of a modern world map you can see that you are in fact only on a small peninsula. The actual dividing point is at Cape Agulhas, the southern tip of the African continent, 150 miles to the south, where we'd been just a few days prior. However, the idea of a "dividing line" between oceans is a rather ambiguous and theoretical idea in my opinion.

Being a weekend and so close to the large and outdoorsy population of Cape Town, Cape Point was very popular, even on a rainy winter day. After enjoying the views with several hundred other people, we moved on to an ostrich farm where we relaxed with some tea, bought a bag of ostrich treats and spent some time feeding the monstrous birds.

Ostriches, a species that is native to southern Africa, have been raised for their feathers here since the 19th century.

We took the scenic route back to Maarten's and caught a breathtaking view of the sun setting over the ocean from high on a hillside overlooking town.

After swinging by his house to grab our bags, Maarten was kind enough to drive us to the far side of Cape Town to the home of our next host, none other than Alicia's husband, Nils. That connection back at Santa Paloma had actually panned out. Alicia was still out-of-town and Nils had graciously invited us to stay with him for several days.

The original arrangement proposed by Alicia was that we could have an air mattress in Finn's room, which was completely fine with us, but when we arrived, we found that Nils planned to take the air mattress himself and put us up in their room instead. He wouldn't take no for an answer and we graciously accepted the over-the-top hospitality of a complete stranger. He also had dinner ready for us when we arrived.

On the road, I was constantly surprised and amazed by the overwhelming kindness and hospitality of strangers and of how miniscule a connection it took to move you beyond stranger to friend.

21. Cape Town, Western Cape, South Africa (Days 99 to 104)

Nils and Alicia lived in a section of Cape Town called Zonnebloem, part of an area formerly known as District 6. District 6 is infamous as the site of the forcible removal of over 60,000 inhabitants by the apartheid regime in the 1970s. In the 1940s the area housed almost one tenth of Cape Town's population and was poor, but diverse and cosmopolitan. The majority of residents were "coloured" Cape Malay and "black" Xhosa, but with a mix of Afrikaners, "whites" and Indians as well. One of the tenets of the apartheid philosophy was that interracial interaction breeds conflict and therefore races should be kept completely separate. Once the Group Areas Act was passed in 1966, the government deemed District 6 a "whites only area" and began to systematically remove residents from this perfectly situated piece of land near the city center, and close to both the harbor and Table Mountain.

FOR USE BY WHITE PERSONS

THESE PUBLIC PREMISES AND THE AMENITIES THEREOF HAVE BEEN RESERVED FOR THE EXCLUSIVE USE OF WHITE PERSONS.

By Order Provincial Secretary

VIR GEBRUIK DEUR BLANKES

HIERDIE OPENBARE PERSEEL EN DIE GERIEWE DAARVAN IS VIR DIE UITSLUITLIKE GEBRUIK VAN BLANKES AANGEWYS.

Op Las Provinsiale Sekretaris

Between 1966 and 1982, 60,000 residents were forcibly relocated to the Cape Flats township 15 miles away, where poverty, gangs and high unemployment still plague residents. The entire District 6 area was bulldozed – except for places of worship, which were oddly preserved – and very little was ever actually redeveloped until after the fall of apartheid in 1994. The government has made some efforts to recognize the claims of former residents, but the success of that process has been questionable and there are still large tracts of completely undeveloped land. On our walks to downtown it was odd to pass by not just vacant lots, but vast fields overgrown with waist-high grasses in the midst of built up neighborhoods.

Interestingly, the events of the 1970s in District 6 are the inspiration for Peter Jackson and Neill Blomkamp's science fiction film "District 9" in which a population of alien refugees are treated as second-class citizens and forcibly resettled to a new area.

Although, we were staying close enough to walk downtown, we also found a bus route on the MyCiTi rapid transit system, which had just started running. Cape Town has really only started coming into its own as a modern, cosmopolitan city since 1994, and things like public transportation which is taken for granted in much of the world still have a long way to go. But then, this is Africa, and compared to other African cities we've seen, Cape Town is amazing in all regards. In so many ways, we suddenly felt that we could be in the U.S. or Europe. There were fancy restaurants, high-end stores, beautiful arks, stunning architecture and even a thriving coffee culture. We really enjoyed and frequented a coffee shop that Nils recommended to us called Truth Coffee, which had decent internet, really good coffee and a steampunk theme.

We visited the District 6 Museum where we learned even more about South Africa's fascinating and disturbing history, and we had lunch with Sharon, an email acquaintance that we had connected with years ago, never really expecting to meet in person. It was turning into a beautiful day and Sharon graciously dropped us off at the cable car station for Table Mountain after lunch.

The cable car is by far the easiest way to get to the top of the mountain although it is possible, albeit quite a bit more labor-intensive, to navigate on foot as well via a network of trails. The view from the top is breathtaking with the city laid out below like a carpet, broken into distinct sections by impassably steep hills, and beyond that, the ocean.

We watched the clouds roll in from the ocean, gradually overtaking the lesser peaks until the view off to one side was just a carpet of clouds. In the direction of the city, the visibility was still clear and we opted to take the paths down instead of the cable car for a different view and a little exercise. In less than an hour we were back on the city streets headed home. It was getting dark and my Africa rule had been not to be out without a group after dark, so we managed to hail a cab for the final mile or two.

Our original plan had been to stay with Nils for three nights, thinking we'd have a flight out to Johannesburg by the third day. Those plans changed for a number of reasons, which I'll get to in a minute, and we were enjoying Cape Town so much that we decided to stay a few more days. We felt like three nights were more than enough for Nils to be on an air mattress in his own home though and we didn't want to overstay our welcome. We made plans to leave the next day, but when we told Nils, he mentioned he'd been thinking of having a braai for us the next night and looked so incredibly disappointed that there was absolutely no way we could leave. We didn't really want to leave and we figured if he was that disappointed to have us leave, we must not be imposing too much.

Braais are a bit like an American BBQ on steroids – like a Fourth of July BBQ, that happens much more frequently - weekly or even bi-weekly. The term itself comes simply from the Afrikaans word meaning "to grill".

Although we'd heard braais mentioned since arriving in South Africa, we hadn't had the opportunity to experience one

247

ourselves. This kind of cultural experience – the things "normal people" do in a place – is our favorite thing about travel. Experiences like this aren't something you can buy so We couldn't say no and gratefully accepted Nils' extended hospitality for another two nights.

Braais are frequently weekend occurrences, but we learned they are also common on Wednesday evenings. Much like the concept of celebrating Wednesday as "hump day" in the U.S., a Wednesday braai can act as a sort of pick-me-up and celebration of making it halfway to the weekend. Never ones to complain about a reason to get together with great people to eat and drink, it seemed like a great concept to us. That afternoon,

Nils came home with at least five different kinds of meat, including ostrich, and got the grilling going. Several friends arrived bearing bottles of wine and the braai was on. I helped to prepare the one and only non-meat offering, a sort of grilled tomato sandwich. This "dish" seemed like an afterthought, like at some point in the evolution of the braai someone thought "oh, we should probably have something besides meat – grilled tomato sandwich, yeah, let's have that too." We'd already thought several times in the past month that South Africa would be a rough place to be a vegetarian, and the braai only reinforced that impression. South Africans seem to love meat, all kinds of meat and there is a wide variety available from wild game steaks to biltong. Biltong is a delicious form of meat – dried, like jerky, but oh so much better. Should you be lucky enough to encounter it, definitely give it a try. We liked the Kudu variety the best.

We had a fantastic evening sitting in the backyard eating, drinking and chatting with the other guests. When we told one woman where we were from, she squealed with delight and exclaimed "Ohhh, I love Americans!" While we were welcomed in all locations, this was certainly one of our most enthusiastic welcomes of the journey, and one I doubt I'll ever forget. We were a bit taken aback at first, but were thrilled; it's not often you are greeted with such warmth and energy. It was wonderful! We were so happy we'd stayed on another few nights.

Because many countries, particularly in Africa, require that travelers crossing their borders have multiple empty pages in their passports, we knew we would need to get some pages added to our passports before going much farther on this trip. We thought Cape Town would be our best opportunity, being a major modern city and early in the African leg of our trip. Once we began investigating how to go about this process, we quickly learned that we needed to make an appointment at the Embassy several days in advance. This meant we wouldn't be able to leave Cape Town for a few more days. We didn't mind this at all, as we were really loving the city. However, while our time with Nils was a highlight of our trip, we were feeling really guilty about kicking him out of his room for so long. We'd already stayed longer than originally agreed, so being conscious about imposing on our very gracious host, we made reservations elsewhere for our last few nights.

From Nils' comfortable home, we moved across town to the Anchor Bay Guest House. Anchor Bay was $40 a night, with a great location and near perfect TripAdvisor reviews. Located high up on the hillside between Table Mountain and the ocean, we had a balcony overlooking the neighborhood of Green Point, the Cape Town Stadium, the Green Point Lighthouse and the Atlantic Ocean. We also found upon arrival that they had a Nespresso machine, which we were free to use to our tastebuds' delight. We drank a lot of espresso in those few days and quickly vowed that when we set up house again, we would have one of these fabulous machines of our very own.

At first light on Friday morning we left the comfort of our guesthouse and headed to the U.S. Embassy for our appointment. When we'd decided that Cape Town would be our best choice for visiting a U.S. Embassy, we assumed that the Embassy itself would be easily accessible. However, instead of being located downtown as anticipated, the Embassy was in a distant suburb. Not having a car, we were relegated to a train/walk/taxi route that proved to be a five-hour roundtrip. The Embassy was in the well-to-do suburb of Steenberg, 18 stops south on the Southern Suburb Line of the Cape Town Metrorail, which took us through some less than well-to-do areas. We'd read some cautionary advice about trains in South Africa, but it seemed this stretch was relatively safe if basic precautions were taken, like not displaying valuables and choosing a full car. I was decidedly nervous about the whole thing but felt that it was a reasonable decision. It was 8 a.m. after all and we really couldn't afford a taxi.

The cars were sparse with a few benches along the walls, and most were all but empty, making it difficult to "choose a full car". Our ride was uneventful. However, when we got off at the tiny Steenberg station we found ourselves in a rundown, largely abandoned-looking area. There were lots of people walking here and there, and not a single taxi.

I was nervous. In fact, the whole trip to the Embassy was a journey that was more than a bit out of my comfort zone. Daryle on the other hand, who is originally from Chicago, was not out of his comfort zone at all. What I saw was a rundown train that landed me in the "hood" where I was likely to be mugged. What he saw, was some urban public transportation and a lot of decent, hard-working Cape Town residents going to and from work. Although I have no way of knowing for sure, I'm relatively certain Daryle was right and I have a lot of growing to do.

After a few minutes, we did notice a taxi office. There was a man in the booth and we asked him how we could get to the Embassy. He immediately offered to take us for 40-rand, a fee he clearly felt to be exorbitant. We tried hard to look thoughtful and a little put out as we agreed to his ridiculous price. Forty rand was about $4US. At this point, I would happily have paid $40US. He took us as far as the gates to the Embassy and I admit I was relieved as we entered the heavily guarded compound.

We produced our passports, went through security and took seats in the waiting room. Our appointment time came and went. Finally, we were called to a window where we were able to speak with a decidedly unfriendly woman who informed us that our appointment was only for dropping off our passports; we'd have to come back on Monday to pick them up. It was 10 in the morning and it had taken us two-and-a-half uncomfortable hours just to get there. This news was unexpected and seemed somewhat unreasonable.

The woman at the window was evasive and non-committal, making it sound like we could possibly get our pages today, but probably not, but she couldn't say for sure. We were willing to wait, even quite a long time, in order to avoid a return trip, but only if there was legitimately a chance we might actually get the pages we needed today.

We were committed to remaining calm and non-confrontational and eventually convinced her to let us talk to someone else. She left and returned with an American diplomat who very helpfully explained that they were only open until noon on Fridays and that adding pages was in fact generally an overnight process, with glue that needed to dry, etc. There was just no way they would be able to get them done for us that day. She was apologetic and understanding, and with the addition of a few key details, like the fact that they closed at noon on Fridays, we clearly understood we really were going to have to come back on Monday. Oddly once the diplomat joined her, the first woman, initially cold and detached, was suddenly warm and friendly in a genuinely helpful, compassionate kind of way.

Even though we didn't get what we really wanted or what we were expecting, we did get a reasonable explanation from a friendly person, which is like half a win, especially in Africa. We found repeatedly that our expectation of understanding what was going on, and why, was a distinctly American expectation.

Since we'd gotten a privately chartered 40-rand ride to the Embassy, we weren't sure how to go about getting back to the station. We'd seen minibus taxis zipping around the streets and decided that was probably our best option. Minibus taxis in South Africa drive a set route picking up and dropping off people along the way. The biggest challenge can be figuring out which route you need, particularly when you are unfamiliar with the area. As usual, we'd be relying a bit on the helpfulness of strangers. We were near a shopping mall in a relatively upscale suburban neighborhood at this point and it was the middle of the day, so felt comfortable to just start walking, watching for minibuses passing by in what seemed like the right direction and trying to flag one down. Finally, one stopped for us.

The gaatjie – the conductor who hangs out the sliding door and collects fares – asked where we were going and thankfully said they could get us back to the train. Their route actually ended at a different train station than the one we'd disembarked at that morning, which turned out to be a very helpful turn of events for our return trip on Monday. In contrast to the nearly abandoned and derelict Steenberg station, the Retreat station, one stop to the North, was a bustling hub with plenty of taxis. Our driver told us which route taxi to look for on our return and wished us a great day. The ride cost us 50 cents.

We were relieved that we'd held off purchasing bus tickets to Johannesburg for that evening and instead extended our reservation at Anchor Bay and had an espresso. We spent our passportless weekend relaxing and continuing to enjoy Cape Town. There was a running/walking trail along the ocean just down the hill from our guesthouse and I couldn't resist going for a run. It was a good run, particularly the first few miles before the rain started and I realized I was lost. I really enjoy running in new places and it was nice to be somewhere I felt comfortable going on a run by myself again. In a practical sense, a run is an effective way get the lay of the land, take in details and make note of places to come back to visit later.

On a more philosophical level, a run allows me to briefly feel like a part of the place, like I belong rather than just being a short-term visitor. Running also gives me a chance to think and to be alone, surrounded by people, but distinctly by myself.

I am not comfortable being the running anomaly, however, as it makes me self-conscious and nervous and cancels out my philosophical reasons for running, so I hadn't run since we left Colorado. Central America and Africa to this point hadn't been particularly encouraging to lone female runners. Cape Town was the first place we'd been since leaving Colorado, where runners were a common sight, and running/walking paths not only existed but were well-traveled.

During our few days in Green Point, we also spent some more time downtown, particularly in Green Market Square. This cobblestone square was built in 1696 and is the center of old Cape Town and the current business district. It's been many things since 1696, including a parking lot, a fruits and vegetable market and even, unfortunately, a slave market. Today it's filled with stands selling clothing, footwear, sunglasses, hand-painted fabrics and all types of souvenir items from the local area and throughout Africa. There are buskers performing music and some rather impressive acrobatics. In addition to assorted tumbling, we saw five men balanced in a complicated L-shape with the top man balanced on his head high above the cobblestone street.

There were plenty of coffee shops and restaurants with outdoor seating in the area and we spent quite a bit of time sitting, people watching and taking it all in. We also did a bit of shopping. It was so difficult, not just here, but throughout our trip, to see all the beautiful handicrafts at amazing prices and not be able to bring them back home with me. Our luggage size precluded much in the way of souvenirs, but I did at least purchase a small cloth painted with a family of elephants that I figured would fit in the bottom of my suitcase.

Never knowing when we'd come across a nice first-run theatre again, we also went to see the new Superman movie at the V & A Waterfront theatre. Daryle loves movies, particularly action and comic-book-based movies, so going to the movies is a regular part of our lives. We didn't see that being on the road should make us miss out, and we'd found that movie theatres, like many familiar things experienced on the road, were still subtly different from place to place. For instance, when we'd gone to see "Ironman" in Cancun, we'd experienced our very first assigned seating at the theater, a trend we hoped would follow us back home to Colorado. (It did.)

In Cape Town, we found that instead of putting butter on popcorn, there was a station with a variety of self-serve flavored salts to add. I'm personally not sure how the salt is supposed to adhere to the popcorn without butter, but perhaps I'm just resistant to change.

What I wasn't prepared for as part of my movie experience was that while I was enjoying the movie, my brain was running a parallel analysis of how the actions and statements of characters would be heard by a person who had never been to the United States and who had met few Americans.

Of course I knew intellectually that the majority of blockbuster movies are made in the U.S. What I'd thought less about was that these movies would therefore have an American bias, or at least be American-centric. Among other things, these movies happen in the U.S., generally feature American heroes and, for good or bad, rely on stereotypes that Americans accept. When I watch movies at home, I am vaguely aware of these things, but on the road I found I was self-conscious about them. Watching Superman, a character and story deeply steeped in American patriotism (I mean, the guy is indestructible and stands for "truth, justice and the American way") in a room full of South Africans felt downright strange to me. In fact, I found myself waiting a little anxiously at times to see if the audience would get a connection or appreciate a joke. As a side note, I'm pretty sure Daryle didn't harbor any of these worries or spend any time overanalyzing a movie about a flying superhero and simply enjoyed the show.

Throughout South Africa we were perplexed at the incredible number of Kentucky Fried Chicken restaurants. At first, we thought maybe South Africans just had a huge predilection for fried chicken, but when we looked into it further, it appears that the reason is rather different and more interesting. KFC has been established in South Africa longer than in most of the world, since 1971, prior to the advent of apartheid sanctions. When the U.S. Congress passed laws banning U.S. companies from owning assets in South Africa in 1987, KFC found ways to keep operating. They divested their 60 company-owned stores to a South African holding company and it was determined that the new laws did not apply to their 120 franchise locations. The company continued to collect administrative fees from those locations though and in 1994 reacquired their divested assets. By this point there were 300 locations. By 2013, there were 736. It feels like there is one on every corner.

Having a much later start, other U.S.-based businesses have been slower to get established, although they are coming on fast and furious now. We witnessed a Burger King in the Green Market Square area that had been opened for over a month and still had a line stretching 50 yards out the front door at lunchtime.

Monday morning, we woke up sadly to our last day in Cape Town and made the trek back to the Embassy to collect our passports. Like our return trip to San Ignacio in Belize, the second time was a breeze.

We left as early as we could since it was a long journey where anything could happen, and this time we had a bus to catch. The trip itself was familiar now, and because of that, far less intimidating. Getting off at the busier train station our taxi driver had shown us made things easy and we felt like we knew what we were doing this time, a big change from our first trip. Our return visit to the Embassy was a completely different experience as well. We were a bit nervous, because on our first visit we needed our passports just to get into the building. This time all we had was a rather unofficial-looking yellow piece of paper with a box check-marked to say we had an appointment.

When we arrived we found a long line. We queued up at a podium outside the building with about 30 other people, until at some point about 20 minutes later, the woman at the podium, recognizing our accent, came over and quietly, but hurriedly asked if we were American. When we told her yes, she chastised us for not telling her, seeming worried that she might get in trouble, all that helpful.

Apparently, being American was an immediate pass to the head of the line. Being Embassy newbies, we had no idea how things worked, and on Friday when we were here, being American hadn't seemed to help us out at all.

Inside, we encountered the same stern-faced woman from Friday. We sighed and followed her instructions to take a seat. She quickly recognized us though, smiled and went to collect our passports straightaway.

Something important we'd learned while traveling and that applies to navigating life in general is that you run into people all the time who have the power to give you what you want or need, or to make life difficult. It's important to remember that they don't have to help you, especially if you are asking for something a little out of the ordinary or outside the rules. No matter how stressed out you are or how important this thing is to you, it is absolutely essential that you remain calm and respectful. I don't know how many times we watched people get belligerent with a customs official, hotel clerk or airline representative, but we never saw it work out in their favor.

22. Cape Town to Bulawayo, Zimbabwe (Days 105 - 107)

We were back in the city, ready to catch our 3:15 p.m. bus with plenty of time. It seemed that most Americans who do visit South Africa also make a trip to Victoria Falls. At our game lodge in KwaZulu Natal, nearly everyone we talked to had plans of heading to the falls after wrapping up their safaris, or had already been to the Falls. However, without exception, they were flying to Livingstone on the Zambia side of the falls. We also wanted to see the Falls, but we had opted for a more adventurous route that was simultaneously slower, cheaper and decidedly less comfortable.

We would start off with an overnight bus to Johannesburg (18 hours), then we'd spend the day in the Johannesburg bus station, take another overnight bus from Johannesburg across the border into Zimbabwe to the city of Bulawayo (16 hours) and end with a final overnight leg on a train to the town of Victoria Falls (12-ish hours), on the Zimbabwe side of the falls.

That is three sequential overnight transports. I'm sure some people can sleep just fine on a bus, but I am not one of them. Although I didn't know that yet, as this was to be my first-ever overnight bus trip, I suspected it might be the case. We were mentally preparing for a long haul.

We started out on our adventure full of energy. We had seats with a good view on the upper level, and the bus itself was nicer than I'd expected. However, even though this was a fairly nice double-decker bus complete with reclining seats and footrests, we didn't get more than a few hours of sleep on our first ride, and even those few hours were not high quality sleep. By the time we rolled into Johannesburg the next morning I was less enamored by bus travel and our enthusiasm was waning. We were exhausted, unmotivated and shackled to our backpacks. Add to that Johannesburg's reputation as a particularly dangerous city, and the repeated warnings we'd read about not walking anywhere as a tourist, particularly near the bus station, and we decided to spend the entire eight hours until our evening bus to Zimbabwe sequestered in the station. This was not a comfortable day. The station was noisy and dirty, had far fewer seats than patrons, and had a long line for a bathroom that had no toilet paper, door latches, soap nor paper towels. Everyone looked as dazed and uncomfortable as we felt. People weren't specifically unfriendly, but there was a strong sense of disconnection, people drawn inside, not engaging with each other and looking out for themselves while coexisting in this crowded space.

When we couldn't stand our seats in the terminal anymore, we visited the Wimpy's, a local hamburger chain, on the second floor, looking for food, a change of scenery and the advertised WiFi. It was nice to sit at a table and we started off just outside the restaurant proper in what would have been a patio seat if we'd been outside. We ordered burgers and discovered no WiFi. When asked, an employee told us we'd have to move inside for the WiFi to work. This didn't seem unreasonable so we moved inside and ordered milkshakes. Still not even a WiFi network visible. Our server told us it should be working and that she would check with a manager. Fifteen minutes later, when there was no change and she had not returned with any information, we flagged her down. She said it should be working and we might need to sit farther back in the restaurant. We were doubtful. The entire restaurant was less than half the size of an average McDonald's, but we moved to a table against the back wall. By this point we were pretty sure we were experiencing yet

262

another case of the African aversion to the word "no." Maybe the WiFi works if you move into the kitchen we joked, as we ordered coffee, because WiFi or no, the seats were still a whole lot more comfortable than out in the terminal. There were still plenty of things to do that didn't require the internet, I reminded myself as I pulled out a book.

Finally, at 6 p.m. we boarded our bus. Ten minutes from the station, still very much in downtown Johannesburg, our bus pulled over and an old beat-up car pulled up. The bus driver and ticket-takers all got off the bus. This seemed like an odd turn of events and I was suddenly unsettled, alert and nervous. Those feelings were quickly replaced with amusement as we noticed that the car was filled to the roof with Styrofoam takeout containers that the bus attendants had begun carrying on board and distributing. When they were finished, every passenger had a box of greasy fried chicken and French fries.

When I was finished eating, I reclined my seat and popped out my footrest. I was exhausted and hoping that just maybe I was tired enough to sleep even in a bus seat. I was, but my blissful slumber was cut brutally short as we arrived at the border at 1:30 a.m. As we stared out the windows bleary-eyed, we were shocked to see a dozen other buses and hundreds if not thousands of people milling about.

In our reading of the travel accounts of others, we learned that African border crossings are notoriously inefficient and occasionally corrupt, and this was our first. I was a little nervous, but being on a bus full of people made me feel more confident, and I expected that crossing the border in the middle of the night would be a relatively unpopular way into Zimbabwe. It was, for tourists, but apparently for Zimbabweans making the trip home from South Africa it was incredibly common.

We unloaded and joined a herd of people from other buses outside two windows where officials were having computer problems. The area we congregated in was outside with no crowd management or guidance, just two large openings in the side of a building, much like a concession stand at a high school football game in the 80s, but much more poorly run. We joined the disorganized mass pressed shoulder to shoulder and gradually shuffled ourselves closer to the windows. Getting our passports stamped took an hour.

Relieved, we loaded back on the bus for a trip through the scales, where we found our vehicle exceeded allowed weight limits. An hour-long process of creative problem-solving and rearranging passengers ensued with several more trips through the scales and lots of negotiating we didn't understand. Finally, after another hour, 10 passengers were unloaded and put in a taxi.

About 4 a.m., we went through the scales a final time, met the weight requirements and drove through the checkpoint where we met up with the taxis and reloaded our passengers. Thinking we were now good to go even if a bit overweight, and maybe about to get a much-needed nap, we had a sinking feeling of disappointment when we stopped yet again another few hundred yards down the road. We quickly realized that the first passport stamp we'd waited an hour for had been just the exit stamp for South Africa, and we were about to disembark yet again to gain entry to Zimbabwe.

Along with a pair from the U.K., the only other tourists on our bus, we were shuffled off to a separate and uncrowded area to get our visa. An hour later, after visiting several different windows for various parts of the process, we had our visa stickers affixed in our passports and headed back to the bus.

When we finally spotted our bus in the sea of vehicles and worked our way through the crowd, we were hurried onboard. It turns out it took longer for the four of us to get our visas than it did the rest of the passengers to get their passports stamped and they were waiting on us. It was now 5:30 a.m. and we held our breath as the bus started moving again. We exhaustedly hoped that there wouldn't be a fourth stop for customs where luggage would have to be unloaded from the roof and underneath compartments. After 10 minutes on the road, we realized with a sigh of relief that we were in luck and finally on the road to Victoria Falls.

23. Bulawayo, Zimbabwe (Days 108 to 110)

By the time we arrived in Bulawayo, 42 hours after leaving Cape Town, we were exhausted. It was 10 a.m. and we dutifully trekked across a town with the most blatant disregard for pedestrian safety we'd ever seen, to the train station where we found a sign announcing that the daily evening train to Victoria Falls was cancelled.

For a moment, we just stood there as our brains struggled to make the shift from simple one-foot-in-front-of-the-other activity to the more complex task of recalculating plans. We had been so focused on just making it to Victoria Falls where we could rest and regroup, that the sudden delay of that goal left us deflated and momentarily off-balance.

It didn't take long to shift to problem-solving mode, however, and our disappointment quickly turned to relief as we recognized the immediate opportunity to rest and recover. We gathered enough brain power to come up with a plan, at least for the next 12 hours. Remembering a decent-looking hotel by the bus station where we'd arrived, we began hauling our packs back though town, dodging cars at each intersection. Arriving at the hotel, we booked a room and promptly went to bed at 3 p.m.

This experience was a reminder that there is perhaps no attribute more critical to successful travel than flexibility. The ability to change course on a moment's notice is invaluable, both for navigating uncertain environments and making the most of a trip.

After several hours of napping, a bath (this hotel had no shower) and some good ol' mac and cheese purchased at a local grocery store and made in our guest room microwave, we felt like mostly-functional human beings again.

When we'd reached the hotel we were interested in nothing but sleep – see Maslow's hierarchy of needs – but now that we were rested, we were ready to interact with people again. We touched base via email with Peter, a friend of a friend who lived in town, making plans to meet up for coffee the following day, before (hopefully) leaving on the evening train.

The world is truly a gigantic and simultaneously very small place. When our trip-planning was in its infancy back in Fort Collins – almost 9,400 miles away – a friend of ours had mentioned having a friend in Zimbabwe. He'd passed along that friend's email address, and I filed it away just in case. When we realized a few weeks prior that we'd actually be passing through his town, we dropped him an email introducing ourselves and proposing coffee. Now that we were in town, all we needed to do was work out the time and place.

At 7:30 the next morning, we were in line at the train station before they opened. The train ride was to be a 12-hour-plus overnight trip with a limited number of two-person sleeping berths available, and we really wanted one of them. After waiting until about 9 a.m. with nothing happening at the ticket window, we saw a man come out looking like he had important news. He announced that if we could check back after 10, they would know if a train would be running that evening and, if so, we could get tickets then. We had scheduled to have coffee with Peter at 10:30, and although we didn't want to miss getting tickets, we also weren't ones to stand up a new friend. We only had email and WiFi as ways to communicate and there wasn't a way to reach Peter short of walking the mile back to meet him at the hotel as planned. We reluctantly left the station and headed

267

back through town. When Peter picked us up, we filled him in. He was pretty confident they wouldn't know anything at 10 that they didn't know now, and 11 or 12 was far more reasonable for any new information, so we agreed he'd swing us by the station after coffee.

After enjoying a cup of coffee together, talking about our lives and our travels, we headed back to the train station about noon. There was now a "train cancelled" sign out front. Peter went in to chat with the guy at the ticket booth about what was going on and our chances for tomorrow. It sounded like there may have been some rock-fall on the tracks that was still being cleared. Nothing too certain, but a fair bit more information than we'd been able to glean on our own in the 24 hours we'd now been in town – being a local seemed to help quite a bit.

Our experiences in Africa in general indicated that people had an aversion to using the word "no" or telling us, as tourists, anything we may not have wanted to hear. Because of this, getting a solid answer often proved difficult, especially if there was a problem. For instance, take the question, "Will there be a train this evening?" when the track is blocked by rock-fall. The honest answer is "definitely not." However, we found the more likely answer to be, "We don't know, please come back in two hours and then we will know", followed by "come back in a few more hours and then we will know", and finally, once you have wasted your entire day running back and forth or waiting in line, the answer will finally be "no, I am sorry there will be no train, please come back tomorrow". We learned that the common African response of "it is no problem", almost certainly meant there was indeed a problem.

Staying a few extra days in Bulawayo itself didn't frustrate me – that actually turned out to be fantastic – but coming back every two hours to check if anything had changed was maddening. I recognize now that this was my choice, to get caught up in this cycle rather than simply enjoying my open-ended time in town. A benefit of traveling slowly and making plans as we went was that we weren't locked into a reservation in Victoria Falls yet, and we still had a few weeks until we needed to be back at the airport in Johannesburg for our flight to Kenya. Although we weren't committed to an itinerary, it was still hard for me to rearrange the plan in my head and to stop worrying about not having "enough time" in Victoria Falls – whatever that meant. Relaxing and going with the flow proved to be a beneficial travel trait I found very difficult to adopt.

In the end, the additional time in Bulawayo was more a blessing than a problem, as we gained far greater insight into "everyday Zimbabwe". Bulawayo was a much less touristy town than what we would experience in Victoria Falls and these "extra days" in town are where I feel like I got a better feel for life here, and where I really fell in love with the country and the people.

With the news that the train would again not be running that evening, Peter offered to take us home to stay with his family and we very gratefully accepted. We enjoyed dinner and the chance to sleep in an actual guest room instead of a hotel or bus seat was wonderful. I will never cease to be amazed by the kindness of strangers or by how little it takes to connect two people, particularly when one is thousands of miles from home.

As we sat on the couch, watching TV, catching up on email and investigating what there was to do in town, it came up in casual conversation that sometimes an email message could take longer to arrive here than you would expect, and that in fact, sometimes it might not arrive at all. I found this unusual and pursued the conversation to find that it was a commonly held belief that the government was screening email communication. Now, I'm not sure email screening on this level is possible, let alone probable, but at this point, I did become extra conscious about what I posted on Facebook or shared in emails. I decided to stick with the facts and hold any opinions that could possibly be construed as critical, until we were back across the border in South Africa – just to be safe. This was a completely foreign feeling for me and the first time we'd been in a country where I found myself censoring my communications for my own safety. Was it necessary? I'm not sure, but it didn't seem like the kind of thing you take chances on.

On one hand, things in Zimbabwe seemed "normal", Peter had a comfortable house, owned a business and traveled to the U.S. on occasion, presumably without incident. We spent time hanging out at a small coffee shop in town where dozens of people worked on laptops, not all that dissimilar to an independent shop at home. The internet, although generally slow, seemed unimpeded and open – no blocked sites or anything like that. On the other hand, in recent years opposition party leaders had been known to be kidnapped, beaten, or turn up dead in strangely coincidental accidents when it appeared they might threaten the ruling party in an upcoming election. Like many poorer countries, particularly in Africa, those in government and those simply living their day to day lives seemed to be two very disparate groups of people. As much as I loved Zimbabwe and all the people I met, it's government made me decidedly nervous.

The next day after breakfast, Peter drove us to his office in town – a roomy, but sparsely furnished and utilitarian set of rooms, like most spaces we'd seen in Zimbabwe – and allowed us to stash our packs while we went back to the train station to once again wait in line, hoping today would finally be the day for our train ride to Victoria Falls.

We'd given up getting to the station at opening time, and strolled in around 9 a.m. As soon as we arrived, we could tell this day was different. There actually appeared to be transactions being made at the ticket window.

We were quickly approached by a pair of young women from Germany who asked if we would be interested in sharing a four-person cabin with them. There were no more two-person cabins available, and they were more comfortable with the idea of sharing a compartment with other travelers. As an "older" American couple, I imagine we seemed like pretty safe companions. We liked the plan as well and agreed immediately. Once our tickets were taken care of, we still had 9 hours until the train would leave. We knew what a drag it was to schlep a pack around, so we offered to introduce our new friends to our "old" friend Peter. We were pretty sure he'd be happy to let them stash their bags in his office for the day as well, so we headed back through town, once again feeling like we were in a game of Frogger at every street crossing. Once all bags were safely stowed, we headed our separate ways for the day. Daryle and I decided to start by checking out the recommended and well-rated Natural History Museum of Zimbabwe.

The museum was low-tech and traditional, but well-maintained and nicely presented. The $10 price tag, like most things in Zimbabwe, seemed a little steep for what you were getting and oddly, there were no photos allowed unless you paid a rather disproportionately large extra fee.

In addition to an extensive collection of local flora and taxidermied fauna that acted as a preview of all the things you could look forward to seeing on a local safari, there was a section covering the history of the country and its traditional cultures. The history was comprehensive, including pre- to post-colonial periods, and was presented in a surprisingly fair-minded way – giving unbiased facts about periods of both native and colonial rule. I was suddenly fascinated with the history of a country I hadn't honestly ever given a second thought.

For me, history class had always seemed dry and disconnected – just a lot of names and dates to memorize. However, once I started traveling, I quickly began to see history as a window to understanding another place and its people – as an explanation for how things are and why – and it became meaningful and fascinating. Travel has also revealed to me that the history I was taught had been woefully incomplete, both in breadth and perspective. I don't remember learning much about Africa or Asia at all and when I did, it was certainly from a white colonial perspective – who owned what and how it was economically important to their empire – with little to no inclusion of the native perspective or culture. I now find myself seeking out local history and doing additional research to learn more.

In the afternoon, we attended a meeting of the Bulawayo Rotary Club. Rotary had proven to be a great connector of people, and we had such a wonderful experience with Rotarians in Guatemala that we were thrilled to find out that Peter was a Rotarian as well. When he invited us to attend one of the local clubs that was meeting that day, we quickly accepted.

In addition to a chance to meet interesting local businesspeople making a difference in their communities and the world, the meeting afforded us a chance to poke around an interesting building we would have missed. The Bulawayo Club, where the meeting was held, was a huge building, that offered lodging and dining as well as space for meetings and events. There was even a snooker room – a game I'd heard of in passing, but had to look up for details. (According to Wikipedia, it's a high-society British game derived from billiards.)

The Club was originally founded in 1895, as a social hub for "colonial gentleman", and their website claims it is a great place for those who "appreciate the splendor and grace of a bygone era." Although certainly romanticizing the colonial period, that description did seem to capture the feeling.

Conveniently located near the central business district of Bulawayo, an effort had been made to retain its original features and ambiance. The building was elegant with impressive architecture, including high ceilings, grand wood-floored ballrooms, rich dark wood paneling, chandeliers, pillars and earthy tapestry rugs. The walls were decorated with nearly life-size painted portraits of European men in colonial-era hunting garb, a mosaic of photos of past and current presidents of the Bulawayo Club and the spoils of big game hunts – including the mounted heads of several Cape buffalo and trash cans made from elephant feet (I assume real, but couldn't say for sure). Along with all the grandeur and elegance, there were also plenty of bare walls and sparsely furnished rooms, giving the feeling that this formerly aristocratic establishment was no longer quite as grand as it once was – a recurring theme we were finding in Zimbabwe.

Later that afternoon, we stopped by the grocery store for some snacks for the train, met up with our German friends and said goodbye to our Zimbabwean host, thankful that fate (or a delayed train, depending on what you believe) had brought us together. In a final benevolent and much-appreciated gesture of friendship, Peter saved us another walk across town with our packs, this time in the dark, and gave us a ride to the train station. The train was scheduled to depart at 7:30 p.m. and left right on time. Well, right on time if you ignore the extra two days.

24. Victoria Falls, Zimbabwe (Days 111 to 112)

Daryle and I enjoy train travel above pretty much any other form of transit. Although it's a bit slower than airplanes and even buses, it's also more relaxed, social and a whole lot more comfortable. The Bulawayo-to-Victoria Falls route was certainly not Amtrak, but it had its own charm.

The train itself, beautiful in the 1950s, was in a state of serious decline. These days the train seemed to operate at a level just a hair above functional. Luckily, functional was all we needed.

The wood-paneled hallways gave the impression of a once stately form of transport, but now, the upholstery was torn, the sinks lacked running water and a fraction of the lights even had bulbs. And this was first class…there was also second class and economy. Our four-berth sleeper had an upper and a lower bunk on each side of the compartment with a center aisle that had a sink (that didn't work) on the window side and a table that lowered into the space between bunks. The bottom bunks converted to bench seats for sitting at the table and the upper bunks folded up against the wall to give headroom.

Oddly, while most things in Zimbabwe seemed ridiculously expensive, the first-class sleeper car we'd splurged on cost a mere $12 per person. For an additional $4 we were able to rent (or hire, as they say in this part of the world) sheets, blankets, and pillows for the night. They were clean, pressed, and in better condition than anything else on the train. The attendant would even make your bed for you if you so desired.

The sleeper room only locked from the inside, but with four of us it was no problem to make sure someone was always in the cabin with our bags.

There was even a dining car which was in excellent condition compared to the rest of the train, although the only dining you were going to do was a cup of coffee or tea. I highly suspect the "coffee" we ordered when we ventured down in the morning was actually tea with a lot of hot milk and that no one wanted to tell us they didn't actually have coffee. (See earlier section about hating to say no.) Regardless, it was warm and tasted decent. It was nice to relax outside of our little compartment and sitting there surrounded by the dark wood paneling and shiny wooden bar, it was easy to imagine what the train might have looked and felt like 50 years ago in its heyday.

Most of the train had a well-worn charm to it; the bathroom however, was significantly less charming and almost a deal breaker, although by the time we realized that, we'd purchased tickets and were already on board – no turning back. Suffice it to say, the restroom near our room was in bad shape.

The room was filthy. The toilet itself was nothing more than a bowl over a hole in the train floor. If you cared to look in the bowl (not recommended), you'd see the train tracks flying by beneath. The floors were wet and covered with tracked in mud. I wasn't particularly interested in actually touching the toilet, but trying to hold a stationary squat while the train bumped and swayed was challenging to say the least. I imagine the aim for men was even worse, hence the disgusting nature of the bathroom floor. I just tried not to let my pant legs touch the ground…

Also the bathroom door didn't lock or even latch, which was true of most doors on the train. So as the train sped down the line swaying from side to side, doors would just fly open at random. Not just bathroom doors, but also the train exit doors that were conveniently located just outside the bathroom. So looking out the no-longer-closed bathroom door, you'd see the trees flying by just 10 feet away from your exposed perch on the toilet.

Despite all of this, I absolutely loved this ride. It was so foreign, so unlike anything I'd done before that it seemed almost too fantastic to be real. The route the train takes travels through Hwange National Park, the largest game reserve in Zimbabwe, complete with lions, leopards, cheetahs, elephants, wild dogs, and all the more common game of southern Africa like giraffes and zebras. Disappointingly, little of the trip took part in daylight, so we didn't see a whole lot aside from the sporadic campfire in the bush.

One of my favorite things and most likely something you would never find in America, because of our preoccupation with legal action, was that I could open the huge compartment windows the whole way and lean my entire upper body out the window to feel the fresh air rushing by while looking up at more stars than I ever knew existed. This was one of the single most memorable moments of the trip for me. I felt wildly free and incredibly blessed and a bit afraid that I may never be able to stop this crazy traveling adventure.

That night, I was lulled to sleep in my top bunk by the gentle rocking of the train. Sometime in the middle of the night I woke and realized we weren't moving anymore. Knowing it was about 2 a.m. and we were far from arriving, I stayed awake a few minutes listening and wondering what was up and then went back to sleep. I'm not sure what happened, but it's apparently not unheard of for the train to hit a buffalo or other large animal, in which case we were told the train would stop while the crew butchered the meat and packed it up to cart home.

When I woke up what I estimate was an hour or two later, we were still not moving. I actually felt relieved. The train was scheduled to arrive at 7:30 a.m. and I felt that was far too early. Now, I thought, we'd probably have time to sleep in, eat breakfast and pack up leisurely before being dumped out in the town of Victoria Falls. I went back to sleep and the next time I awoke we were cruising along with sunlight pouring through the window. We spent the next few hours lying in bed, watching the African bush roll by.

From the time the train started to pull into the station at about 10 a.m., we could already see the mist of Victoria Falls in the distance. I'd read the spray can be visible up to 50 miles away and once we saw the falls in person, that was easy to believe. Victoria Falls is alternately known by its Lozi name throughout Zambia and much of Zimbabwe – Mosi-oa-Tunya, which fittingly means "The Smoke that Thunders."

No matter what you call them, the falls are impressive, stretching 5,603 feet across with water falling 324-feet at the highest point. UNESCO says it is the "largest curtain of falling water in the world." In the high water season, up to 132 million gallons of water fall per minute. These falls are massive, so I wasn't prepared for the fact that the points where the falls are actually visible are very limited.

There is really no way to see them except from within one of the national parks on either side of the Zimbabwe/Zambia border, and of course by air. Even though the falls are both tall and wide, they crash into the very deep and narrow Batoka Gorge. It's like all that water just disappears into a tiny crack in the earth. There is virtually no way to get a view of the falls from a distance, except from the air, and even once you are inside one of the national parks, you are so close you aren't actually able to view the entire falls at once.

While we generally tend to be pretty cheap travelers, we opted to make an exception for a helicopter ride over the falls. It was without question the right decision. The helicopter ride lasted 12-13 minutes and cost $140 per person, way outside our budget. However, this was another example of asking a version of the question that got us out the door in the first place, "Will we be more likely to regret spending the money or missing the opportunity?" Given the amount of effort, time and money we'd spent just to get to Victoria Falls, the cost of the helicopter ride paled in comparison.

From the helipad, we flew downstream over the wide braided channel of the Zambezi River until we could see the mist rising up in front of us, and suddenly we were looking over the edge of the falls. It wasn't until this moment that we really got a hint of the full scale of the falls.

From the air you don't get to feel the mist generated by the powerful falls forcing its way up out of the canyon or hear the crashing of the water, but you do get to see the entire falls at once, and you can see the massive scale of the rocky crevasse the falls pour into. The combination of the view from the air and the ground gave us the chance to appreciate both the scale and the power of the falls. The view from the air was worth every penny.

25. Chobe National Park, Botswana (Day 113)

In addition to seeing the falls, we took advantage of our proximity to Botswana to add a safari daytrip and see another country, even if only briefly. The day we spent in Chobe National Park in Botswana was one of the most memorable of the trip.

It was a relatively short trip across the border to Chobe – another fun stamp in the passport, but an efficient and quick one this time – and then a riverboat safari in the morning and jeep safari in the afternoon.

The riverboat safari gave us a hint at how different two safaris can be. In South Africa, we'd been on a fenced game reserve with limited populations of animals and we largely saw one group or type of animals at a time. Chobe has one of the largest concentrations of game in Africa, and the section of the park we saw on this safari was floodplain, so there wasn't a lot of tall vegetation and we could see clearly for thousands of yards. Before we even left the dock we saw a crocodile, almost immediately followed by a pod of hippos and a few elephants along the shore. At times we could see Cape buffalo, hippos, elephants, impalas and crocodiles along with an unbelievable array of birds – all at once.

I was excited to finally see some crocodiles. Not only did we see crocodiles, but we got absolutely as close as I ever care to be to a crocodile. Being on the boat, we could pull up to shore and lean over the rail to get a good look, putting us not more than six feet from some truly huge reptiles.

Chobe National Park is home to 50,000 (or depending where you get your information, maybe as many as 120,000) Kalahari elephants, the largest species of elephant in the world, making it likely the highest concentration of elephants in all of Africa. This is especially impressive as the population has been built up from just a few thousand in the 1990s, while elsewhere in Africa elephant numbers have been shrinking dramatically.

Our impression of Botswana, admittedly formed in only about eight hours, was of a country that has managed its natural resources, economy, and tourism impressively well, a seeming anomaly in Africa. There has been attention paid to development of resources in ways that help to sustain both those resources and the people who live there, rather than exploiting the resources or selling them to the highest bidder. Botswana appears to somehow have escaped the corruption that seems to run rampant in African governments and to have given their people a decent standard of living. We want very much to visit again to learn and see more.

The Chobe River in this portion of the park is a major watering hole for large breeding herds of elephants, especially in the dry season (May – October). We were there in July and we saw so many elephants I still dream about it. If you love elephants, Chobe should certainly rank high on your list. At one point our boat floated on the river less than 50 yards out while a herd of 18 elephants of all sizes, from waist-high babies to 12-foot towering giants, wandered out of the brush. They ambled down to the water's edge and we watched for 10 or 15 minutes while they slowly scooped up gallons of water with their trunks and drank their fill. It is an experience that still today I have to remind myself was real and not the dream it seems like when I think about it from my couch in Colorado.

Along with holding the purring serval kitten and leaning out the train window in the middle of the night in the Zimbabwean bush, this is among my very favorite memories of the trip and quite honestly of my life so far. I know I keep adding to that list, but Africa was really and truly an amazing place – not just on occasion, but on a daily basis. Every time I thought there couldn't be more, there was something unexpected and mind-blowing around the corner.

When the elephants were hydrated, they turned and wandered back into the brush. You would be amazed at how fast an entire herd of the largest land animals on earth can completely disappear.

After a really nice lunch at the safari lodge, we hopped in a Land Cruiser for our second safari of the day. We saw the standard giraffes, impalas and zebras along with a few new critters including a "mob" of banded mongooses, troops of baboons and a small handful of the hundreds of bird species that call Chobe home, including some of the most brilliantly colored I've ever seen.

At one point we were on a hillside overlooking the misty expanse of floodplain and saw a herd of about 20 elephants, again ranging from genuinely tiny calves less than 3 feet tall to humongous giants, crossing the braided channel of the Chobe River. It was a perfect African scene, the unreal kind from movies, but right there in front of me.

As we drove the final stretch back to the lodge to meet our bus back to Zimbabwe, we saw yet another herd of elephants, this time up close, crossing the road right in front of us. We stopped, but one of the elephants who had yet to follow his family across the road hesitated and stopped about 20 feet off to the side of our truck.

All I could do was hold my breath and stare as this 5-ton creature stared back at me and deliberated about what to do next. The elephant rocked back and forth a bit, threw some dirt on his underside, and in a decidedly goofy and playful-looking move, laid his trunk over one of his tusks. We'd seen angry elephants, and this guy looked very much at ease. Even at ease, however, I found an elephant at 20 feet to be paralyzingly terrifying. I found myself unable to talk or move, never mind take a photo. Luckily Daryle, retaining his wits, had observed my paralysis, plucked the camera out of my hands and got a fantastic video of all of this.

After 5 or 10 minutes that seemed like years, our giant new friend ambled across the road to join his buddies and we carried on. So many elephants in one day...I could not have been happier. It should be noted that paralyzing fear and complete joy are not mutually exclusive.

26. Victoria Falls, Zimbabwe - Part II (Days 114 to 118)

Our trip to Victoria Falls had so far included not only the falls and the train, but my first helicopter ride and a breathtaking day in Botswana with dozens of elephants. The next day we added an elephant safari. This is a prime example of what I mean by Africa upping the ante on a daily basis.

Riding an elephant hadn't even made my bucket list. It probably would have if I had realized it was an option. I knew smaller Asian elephants were frequently ridden and used for hauling heavy things like felled trees in Asia, but their larger African cousins were less easily trained, and for the most part this wasn't even attempted.

We'd found a safari company called Wild Horizons that was well-rated and seemed responsibly run. Their elephants have an interesting history. In the 1980s the Zimbabwe Department of National Parks had a policy of culling "excess" animals from within national parks. Frequently those animals were elephants and the approach was to destroy entire herds, with the exception of juveniles, which they would then sell to farmers, zoos or circuses. I know, sad!

Being hand-raised by humans, these juvenile elephants were completely acclimated to people. Because of this acclimation to humans, they couldn't be returned to the wild – they'd most likely have found their way into a town or village and wreaked havoc.

Those that ended up on local farms often escaped and did just that.

One local farmer had an idea. He thought that taking one more step and actually training the elephants might make them easier to handle and useful in the local tourism market. Everyone thought he was crazy, but he succeeded, becoming the first man to successfully train an African elephant in Zimbabwe. When he approached Wild Horizons with the proposal to use the elephants in their tourism operations, they were understandably skeptical. However, they decided to give it a go, as long as the welfare of the animals remained the highest priority and in 1997 they moved the small herd of four elephants to their property.

Wild Horizons is now recognized in the region as an elephant sanctuary for orphaned and abandoned elephants. Today their herd has grown to 23 elephants – all orphaned, abandoned or born into the herd. Each elephant is ridden a maximum of two hours a day and participates daily in reward-based training to reinforce the human-elephant bond. The rest of the time, the elephants are free to roam wild, encountering other animals including other wild elephant herds and returning of their own free will.

When we arrived at Wild Horizons, we were directed to a raised platform and a small collection of elephants lined up around the edge where we could pet their heads and trunks (and take photos of course). During this time, I felt drawn to a female elephant named Janet and chose her as our safari guide.

After getting acquainted, we walked around to a set of steps and climbed into the giant throne-like seat on Janet's back behind our human guide. Janet had a calf who stuck close throughout the ride, stopping periodically to nurse. It was a bit like a horseback ride, but then again, not like that at all. It was thrilling each time I looked back and saw the elephant train behind us crossing the creeks and navigating the bush. This was a pinch-me moment, where I had to remind myself that this was really happening, and I wanted to remember it forever.

The view from so high up was unique, as we moved through the trees, well above the brush. We were almost eye level with the handful of giraffes we saw. The whole elephant "safari" was a bit of a misnomer as we saw few animals, but that was fairly unimportant as we were sitting on the back of an elephant!

Is it comfortable to ride an elephant you might wonder? While on the ride it wasn't noticeably uncomfortable, but that was likely because I was too enamored with being on an elephant's back. When we got off, my legs were completely asleep and I about collapsed when I hit the ground.

Afterward we got to thank Janet and her little one by placing huge handfuls of food into the end of their trunks. They were even trained to wave goodbye with their trunks. It was very sweet and made me want to hug an elephant. While that wasn't possible, I was thrilled to have gotten so close.

As if this experience weren't enough, when we had finished feeding our elephants, we heard there was a surprise. When we returned to the deck, there was a cheetah there to greet us. The cheetah was attentively staring through the railing at some critters in the distance down by the river as we approached.

It did concede to sit up and pose for photos with us. Seeing as how people pay significant amounts of money to go on specific trips for a photo op with a cheetah, having it thrown in as a bonus was an impressive surprise addition to our already amazing elephant safari.

Wild Horizons is big on research and education, and this cheetah was described to us as an ambassador animal – one that frequently goes to schools for show-and-tell of sorts, making sure kids grow up knowing about the majestic animals they share their environment with so they can learn to appreciate and protect them.

As we stepped up for our photo op, we were carefully instructed to be careful not to step on the cheetah's tail, to which I thought, "You need to tell us that?!" After we had our photo snapped, I stepped backward to walk calmly away from the cheetah and narrowly missed his big fat tail. My blood pressure spiked, my heart raced and I am now sure they warn you because it's happened, probably more than once. I hate to think what kind of reaction that would evoke. I've accidentally stepped on my very tiny kitty's tail and even that was incredibly unpleasant for all involved.

We were coming to the end of our time in Victoria Falls and later that afternoon decided to find the "Big Tree" we'd seen marked on the town map. Disconcertingly, as we explored the forest along a small river on the way to the tree we saw very large footprints. Unmistakably elephant footprints. This was the first time we'd been on our own, on foot, in a place where there were clearly wild elephants about. I can assure you this is an exhilarating, but scary and very foreign feeling.

We mostly stayed on the dirt road after this and kept a close eye out. I don't know what I would have done if we'd actually spotted elephants close by, but I figured they were like bears, in that surprising them was probably a bad idea.

The trip to the tree was several miles round-trip and we saw no other walkers and only a few cars. The tree was indeed very big and very old. The sign told us this baobab was 1,000-1,500 years old, 60 feet around and 75 feet tall.

At this point, we needed to get on to Kenya, where we were scheduled to start a month-long volunteer commitment, but the only reasonable place to catch a long-haul flight out of this part of Africa was to get ourselves back to Johannesburg. That meant a return journey on the train to Bulawayo and an overnight bus back across the border to Johannesburg.

The train was again an overnight train, so we had some time to kill before our 7:30 p.m. departure. We stopped by the grocery store to stock up on some travel food. At the checkout we paid for our purchases with U.S. dollars. The checker handed us a few bills as change and then offered us lollipops for the difference, saying they didn't have any coins. There are some downfalls as a country, to not having your own money. Since 2009 when inflation got totally out of hand, Zimbabwe has been using American currency and South African coins. Sometimes they run out.

After taking three lollipops, we were approached by a man who asked us if it was true that in America you could get as much bread as you wanted for $1. We were perplexed by this question, answering that you could indeed get a loaf, maybe even two, for a dollar, but not an unlimited quantity. That's just not how buying things works. This was a lesson in perceptions. Where he got this idea from we'll probably never know, but it was enlightening to know such ideas were out there. It was a humorous look at how all kinds of perceptions proliferate in the absence of actual knowledge. Unfortunately, this phenomenon is frequently not as humorous nor benign.

During this time, we also did some souvenir shopping and bought a dozen or so carved necklaces, some to keep and others for gifting to upcoming hosts. Because it was a design unique to the region, we bought several necklaces with carvings of Nyaminyami the Zambezi River God, depicted with the body of a snake and the head of a fish.

Nyaminyami is one of the most important gods of the Zambian Tonga people and is believed to protect them and provide for them in difficult times. Carved images of Nyaminyami were everywhere. Being so unique to the area and so inexpensive and small made them the perfect gifts and souvenirs. Even once we were on the train, someone showed up offering more Nyaminyami necklaces through our carriage window. We bought 5 more for a dollar, by far the cheapest price yet.

Legend has it that Nyaminyami lived under a large rock that stuck out into the Zambezi River near the current location of the Kariba dam, several hundred miles downstream from Victoria Falls. If people navigated too close to the rock in their canoes they'd get sucked under in whirlpools and, the Tonga believed, dragged down to spend eternity under the water.

When the dam was constructed, trees were bulldozed and housing for workers was built along the river; the Tonga people were forced to resettle away from the river. When the dam was finished the water level had risen 30 feet, covering the large rock and angering Nyaminyami. Even worse than the water rise, local people believe Nyaminyami was married and that he and his wife were separated by the building of the dam. It's mythology, but during the building of the Kariba dam between 1950 and 1958, the river did experience four unprecedented and catastrophic floods, costing the lives of 80 construction workers. Today when there are mild earth tremors, locals claim that it is Nyaminyami coming up to the dam in an attempt to see his wife. The Tonga people believe that one day Nyaminyami will destroy the dam and they will be returned to their original pre-dam home along the river banks.

The train station is near the The Victoria Falls Hotel, Zimbabwe's oldest luxury hotel built by the British in 1904. We decided that enjoying high tea on the patio overlooking the beautifully manicured hotel grounds with the mist from the falls visible in the distance was a fitting way to close this chapter of our adventure. For anyone who has not enjoyed "high tea" or thinks "that's really not my thing," you need to understand that it is not about the tea as much as it is about the food. All kinds of small finger foods from tiny sandwiches to minute pastries arranged on a three-tier cake stand. Of course there's tea as well, but it's so much more than that, and you will not leave hungry.

On the train ride back to Bulawayo, I thought a lot about this fascinating and beautiful country and its gracious, optimistic people who had truly grabbed my heart. Zimbabwe is a relatively new independent nation having gained independence only in 1980.

After colonization by the British in the late 1800s and early 1900s, Zimbabwe, then known as Rhodesia, became a self-governing British colony in 1922. In 1964 the white minority government declared itself a republic. This didn't go over well with the British or indigenous Zimbabweans. Britain chose to ignore things, but this kicked off a long civil war between Ian Smith and his white minority government, and opposing "rebel" group leaders Joshua Nkomo and Robert Mugabe. After a long civil war, independence was made official in 1980 with a grand, well-attended celebration complete with a rendition of "God save the Queen". In attendance was Charles, the Prince of Wales, Indira Gandhi (prime minister of India at the time) and the prime ministers or presidents of Nigeria, Botswana, Zambia and Australia (as a representative of the Commonwealth of Nations). Bob Marley even performed a song he'd written specifically for the occasion at the request of the government, entitled "Zimbabwe."

At this time Mugabe was named the country's first prime minister in British-supervised elections. Thirty years later, after several less convincingly fair elections, Mugabe remained the country's ruler. (In 2008, he actually narrowly lost the first-round election, only to win the required runoff election in a landslide when his opponent dropped out citing widespread violence and intimidation.) During his rule, Mugabe had been doing quite a bit of work increasing the power of his party and the government in general, and also doing a lot of amending to the constitution.

Initially things went OK but by the mid-1990s the country was in economic crisis. Around this time the government began a program of forcible land distribution to try to redistribute the large percentage of white-owned farmland to indigenous black Zimbabweans. The government ordered the police and military not to stop the invasion and takeover of white-owned farms. With no consequences and no one to stop them, a number of disenfranchised citizens began taking over farms using intimidation and violence. Predictably this was followed by a mass emigration of white Zimbabweans to South Africa and abroad.

Unfortunately, the people forcibly taking over the farms were not really interested or experienced in farming – they were just interested in the taking part. Zimbabwe has a large amount of arable land and today almost none of it is growing anything. Once the "breadbasket of Africa," Zimbabwe became one of the most food-insecure countries in the world. The people of Zimbabwe have endured repeated economic crises, food shortages, unreliable water and electricity supplies, a cholera outbreak and incredible inflation. From 2000-2007, the economy shrank 50% and in 2007 inflation peaked at 8,000%. Inflation was so out of control that shops would have to reprice goods multiple times a day to keep up. At one point Mugabe slashed three zeros off the end of the currency just to make it more manageable.

In the town of Victoria Falls, someone on the street would approach us roughly every 10 minutes wanting to sell us a set of the now defunct Zimbabwean currency. The top ranking bill was a trillion-dollar note. They offered to sell the whole set of bills including this trillion-dollar bill for $2US. When we were there, the Zimbabwean currency was no longer in circulation and they were using a combination of the oldest U.S. currency you will ever see and South African rand coins. The ATMs dispensed American bills that were so well-worn they felt like cloth you had repeatedly polished shoes with, and $2 bills were common.

And yet, despite all the hardship, the people we met in Zimbabwe were unfailingly friendly and optimistic. Black and white, they loved their country. And they should, it was beautiful! There were still free-roaming elephants, Victoria Falls was one of the seven natural wonders of the world on nearly any version of that list, and looking out the windows of the train from Bulawayo to Victoria Falls I saw more stars than I knew existed. When you think of the African bush, Zimbabwe is probably what you are picturing.

I spent a lot of time wondering how this country could possibly be functioning. There was such a huge disconnect between the cost of goods and the income of the average people. The availability of goods was certainly far less than we were used to in America and the prices on what was available were often even higher than in the U.S. The pay for the average worker was nowhere near the United States. For instance, a barber in Bulawayo might only make $2 cutting your hair, but he'd still pay $50 to buy a basic blanket at the store down the street. On top of that, unemployment was upwards of 70% by most accounts, maybe even as high as 95% (although the government would have had you believe it was below 10%). Yet, unlike next door in South Africa, crime didn't seem to be that much of a problem.

I wondered how this scenario could be remotely sustainable. It started to make a bit more sense when I learned that of the 13 million people who call Zimbabwe home, it was estimated that about 4 million were working outside the country and sending money back. Our experience at the border certainly supported this estimate. There were dozens, probably hundreds, of buses to and from South Africa daily and most, if not all, were primarily filled with Zimbabweans. Even at 3 a.m., when we crossed the border into Zimbabwe there were at least a dozen other buses.

I'd wager ours was the nicest and we still had only four tourists onboard; the rest had Zimbabwe passports.

The general feeling we got in Zimbabwe was that things were quite nice once but have been in decline for some time. I had to wonder how long this decline could continue without more drastic consequences. How long could a country keep forcing its people to leave in order to make a living? And how long could the people continue to be optimistic?

In 2013, only a few weeks after we left Zimbabwe, Mugabe won a seventh term with a 61% election victory. Fairly? Few people think so.

As I write this, Zimbabwe is in the news for continued economic decline and I keep wondering how the country is changing and how the people are handling it.

Back in Bulawayo, we grabbed bus tickets for the evening bus to Johannesburg and spent the afternoon at the trendy and comfortable coffee shop Peter had introduced us to. When we arrived in Johannesburg at 6 a.m. the following morning, we took the Gautrain to the airport and waited for the first of four flights that would take us to Watamu, Kenya, over the next 24 hours, where we were scheduled to spend the next month volunteering.

27. Watamu, Kalifi County, Kenya – A Rocha (Days 119 to 141)

We knew we'd be arriving in Mombasa at 6 a.m. on very little sleep and in a moment of clear-thinking genius, we'd actually ordered a cab to meet us at the airport instead of trying to navigate several legs of unfamiliar local public transport in a country we knew very little about. The trip to Watamu was an hour and a half by "taxi," and I can only imagine how long it might have taken us by tuk-tuk and matatu (privately owned minibuses commonly used in Kenya as route taxis).

Cabs in Kenya are not so much taxis as you think of them in, say, New York; here they're more like a friend of a friend who picks you up at the airport for money, like Uber without the app. In this case it was $150 (or two days' budget as it was known to us.) It was a hard amount to part with, but as we drove around roundabout after roundabout through pitch black streets of run-down buildings and rush-hour-like foot traffic, I have never been so glad to not have taken the frugal route.

Having no idea where we were, how to get where we were going or who the person driving us was, it seemed prudent to stay awake and alert. However, no matter how hard I fought it, I kept dozing off and, ultimately, I decided we would end up where we ended up and that paying attention wouldn't really make much difference. As usual, or really always so far, people proved to be trustworthy and good and we arrived on the doorstep of our bed and breakfast in Watamu just after 10 a.m. Our gracious Italian hosts offered us coffee, which we accepted, and let us check in right away. We went straight to bed for six hours, caffeine be damned, only getting up to go in search of dinner.

I was again thankful for Daryle's penchant for advocating for "rest days," as we were able to spend several days sleeping a lot and wandering around town to get the lay of the land before starting our volunteer engagement. During these few days, we learned that our Italian hosts were not an anomaly and that the Kenyan coast from Mombasa to the border with Somalia has been a popular vacation destination for Italians for some time. Not only that, but a significant number have chosen to call the area home, leading to a curious dynamic where Italian was spoken as widely as English or Swahili and the default greeting on the street, even from a native Kenyan, seemed to be "Ciao."

Finally on August 1, we checked into our guesthouse and volunteer accommodations for the next month. Our time in Kenya was a big switching of gears. Daryle and I had been together nearly 24/7 since leaving Colorado and had rarely stayed in any place more than a few days since leaving Sayulita. It was a nice change of pace to have meaningful, longer-term interactions with other people. And while we love being together, Kenya gave us an opportunity to attend to our differing needs for social interaction. Daryle got to carve out some much-needed alone time and I got to take advantage of our oceanfront location, indulging in all kinds of water activities that Daryle had no interest in, with new water-loving friends.

Since we were there to volunteer, a second sort of shift occurred as well. This one was a bit more challenging for me. I suddenly felt a sense of responsibility to someone else that had been lacking for a number of months.

I had signed us up to volunteer and I was here to work. However, my people pleasing mind was into that commitment far more than my free-spirited heart when we arrived and my planner nature was frustrated by the lack of a clear job description and expectations.

I was the one who had been dead-set on volunteering at some point in our trip, feeling like if we were going to travel for this long, we should at least spend a small amount of time doing something useful and good for the world. This is what I'd settled on.

The organization I'd chosen to work with is called A Rocha, a U.K.-based Christian organization that engages local communities in conservation. They are active in 19 countries and focus on scientific research including ecological monitoring, community-based conservation and environmental education. Mwamba, where we were staying, is the residential field study center of A Rocha Kenya. In addition to the guesthouse for volunteers and visitors, the center also serves as the local offices, so Monday through Friday it was the base of operations with employees coming and going, in addition to the small collection of rotating volunteers and visitors living onsite.

Knowing that being in Kenya was my choice and we were here "for me", I felt pressure to enjoy what I was doing, to be useful to the organization, and for this to be a formative life-changing kind of experience. Basically, I needed to feel the time was "worthwhile", whatever that meant. Two days in, it became apparent there was no real plan for what I was to be doing and I spent the next several days rushing from possibility to possibility, quickly voting one down and moving on until I'd exhausted all the options and found myself no closer to a satisfactory solution.

In the end, the experience did turn out to be revelatory, but in very different ways than I expected.

Initially, I thought the combo of an NGO and a conservation organization would be perfect, and that I might be able to contribute both scientifically and organizationally. When I left my job in nonprofit fundraising with an organization working with at-risk youth, I'd been dreaming about "returning to my roots" so to speak and heading in a direction more in line with the biology and ecology degrees I'd worked so hard to obtain. I missed the analytical nature of science and the hands-on experience of being in the field.

I'd talked to some of the staff biologists at A Rocha before embarking on our journey and they were encouraging and excited to have my experience. I expected there to be some idea of what to do with me when I turned up based on those conversations, but the ball turned out to be way more in my court than I expected, and the person I'd had most of those conversations with wasn't even in the country.

I also quickly realized that I was far less certain of what I wanted out of the experience than I'd thought. As the center director and an onsite grad student working on his Ph.D. started trying to help me find a place to fit in for the month, I rapidly discovered several things: a) my fascination with all things associated with tropical reefs was more romantic than practical, b) I didn't have the basic familiarity with local ecosystems to pose a reasonable hypothesis or develop a useful, well-informed research project on my own, certainly not one I could conceive and complete within a month, and c) I really don't love research enough to be a scientist. I probably should have remembered discerning this third point the first time, 11 years earlier when I was half-way through my Master's degree in Ecology.

Sometimes you think you've changed over time with additional experiences and knowledge, only to realize you are actually quite the same person you were then, and that you are reliving a dilemma you already worked through once.

This process of coming to terms with reality all sounds very rational as I write about it, like I reasonably thought through all of my reactions and emotions. This is not, however, a very complete picture of the process. If you asked Daryle, he'd tell you I spent the first several days in a frenzied state of freak out – and he'd be correct.

For the first four days at Mwamba, I couldn't think about anything but figuring out what my purpose was there and what I needed to accomplish. I couldn't enjoy myself. The fact that I felt the clock was running didn't allow me to stop and think either, it just whipped me into a greater frenzy. I felt I had to get to work immediately, but I didn't have any idea what that work was. The decision of what to focus on for the month was largely up to me, but I couldn't decide what to act on. This overwhelming feeling of helplessness and indecision took me by complete surprise.

I felt I'd made a huge mistake, wasting an entire month of the trip, and wondered if we should bail before we wasted more time. I cried. I made Daryle listen to hours of indecisive circular reasoning. I took walks on the beach that turned into runs because I learned no one talks to you or tries to sell you anything if you are running. And then, on day 5, I suddenly recovered my senses.

I came to terms with the fact that I wasn't going to change the world with a month of volunteer work, and that was OK. I realized this wasn't going to be the moment that changed the course of my professional life, and that was OK too. While contributing something worthwhile to A Rocha was important, so was embracing the experience of being in Kenya and learning as much as I could in the short amount of time we'd be there.

My unprecedented and frankly unwarranted meltdown taught me a lot about myself as well. I learned that when faced with a relatively long period of uncertainty, I tend to freak out. Good to know. And apparently "a long period of time" to me starts at one month.

I have now learned to recognize this irrational state when it occurs, and taught myself to channel our Mexican guide, Jorge, repeating over and over our travel mantra, "Don't Freak Out," while waiting for the panic to subside. I also know that I need to refrain from making any serious decisions until that happens. I hate to think about all the experiences I would have missed out on if we'd bailed out and left Mwamba one week in. I learned that I need to take one day at a time doing the best I can and not judge myself, until one day I wake up and realize everything is in fact OK. Once my reasonable self is once again in charge, I am allowed to start making decisions again.

In hindsight, I see that I learned a far greater lesson as well. I realized that in many cases far more can be gained by being open to experiences than by having a set goal or plan. Yes, I helped A Rocha out a little in my month, but the experiences I had and the people I met changed me far more than I impacted anything. The majority of these experiences and relationships were unplanned and unexpected but caused me to develop a broader, more realistic and balanced view of the world. These experiences continue to shape how I view and interact with the world today, and I would have missed them if I'd been too focused on what I had to share to be open to exploring and learning myself.

319

In the end, despite my initial internal vehement opposition, I ended up doing what my more recent skill set lent me to and the area that all nonprofits the world over are all too happy to accept help with — fundraising.

I spent a good bit of my time working on setting up an online donor database, and Daryle worked on their website (another skill set useful anywhere). The only problem with this was that from the time everyone arrived at the office around 8 in the morning until dinner time at about 6, the internet was so painfully slow it was often literally impossible even to check email, never mind internet research. Frequently, it wasn't even possible to load the most basic websites. I tried to do as much online work as possible before breakfast, after dinner and on the weekend, with writing and word processing during "peak times." I also repeatedly reminded my rule-based, type-A self that I was in Kenya for probably the only time in my life and, despite my commitments, I should make sure I was taking advantage of once-in-a-lifetime opportunities and enjoying myself as well.

When I look back, I think I did well in that quest for balance. Every morning, I had no idea what opportunity would present itself, but I knew I was going to say yes.

I kayaked beyond the reef over huge swells, snorkeled with sea life so colorful it was beyond what I'd dreamed existed, and spent an entire day on shore with binoculars surveying whales for a local conservation organization. One day, I ran down to the beach by our guest house just in time to witness sea turtles, caught accidentally by local fishermen, being released back to the ocean by the local marine conservation organization.

The large number of exotic and captivating, but locally common critters we saw in their native habitat was a highlight for me. We had monkeys playing on the clotheslines outside our room. Tiny frogs and stick insects showed up around the guest house, and one night Benjo, a Ph.D. student from the United Kingdom, came into the living/dining room with a hedgehog he'd just picked up outside rustling around in the bushes.

I was reminded every day that the world we were inhabiting was vastly different from the one I was used to. These reminders were overwhelmingly positive, but occasionally were pointed out in more appalling and less OK ways.

Kenya is home to 127 species of snakes. Like most places, the majority won't hurt you, at least not seriously, but here there are 24 that could kill you. You've probably heard some of their names – puff adders, black mambas, green mambas, along with the world's largest species of spitting cobra (up to 9 feet long). You get the idea. It was a different kind of snake encounter though that gave me a very distinct "I'm not in Kansas anymore" moment.

It was a quiet Sunday afternoon at Mwamba and we were sitting around chatting and playing cards when a phone call came from the wife of the Mwamba director, who lived about a mile down the beach. Her husband was out of town and she was calling for help. She had heard some disturbing noises coming from the backyard and one of their Jack Russell terriers was not responding when called. She was pretty certain he had just been swallowed by a rock python. My first thought? WTF?!

It turned out that was exactly what had happened. The 16-pound dog that had just yesterday been barking jubilantly and tearing around the Mwamba property was now a big lump in the belly of an unimaginably huge snake.

The North African rock python, also known as the coast python, is Africa's largest snake and can be up to 20 feet long. Up until that moment, I was blissfully unaware that anything that huge and reptilian was lurking in the coastal forest we were living in.

Since Watamu is home to the Bio Ken Snake Farm, a reptile research center, we immediately placed a call to them. While they sent someone over, several of our group hopped in the truck to meet them.

I imagine a snake that has just had the equivalent of Thanksgiving dinner gets a bit sluggish and (although I wouldn't recommend this course of action without trained snake handlers) it turns out that when stretched out lengthwise, even a python is not that strong and can be wrangled into a burlap sack. Despite the catch, unfortunately there was no recourse for Jonge, the Jack Russell terrier. Once swallowed by a snake, whole or not, there's not much that can be done.

This was an unexpected experience that I had no frame of reference for. That's how so many of my experiences in Africa, good and not as good, were. Incomparable. Things happened every day that were so far out of my comprehension that I had to take several steps back to rethink my worldview.

28. Watamu, Kenya - People

Kenya wasn't all animals and outdoor adventures. Being at A Rocha offered us many opportunities to get a glimpse into the local community and culture as well, sometimes directly and other times just as a product of being in the area in a less touristy way and location.

In Watamu we also experienced unimagined connections and the chance to see what everyday life looked like for a variety of Watamuans. (I have no idea if that's how they refer to themselves. I doubt it, but I liked the way it sounded.)

Just two days into our time at Mwamba, we attended the very first meeting of the newly chartered Watamu Rotary Club where we met Priscilla and Japheth, a couple who ran a local restaurant as well as a program for the orphaned children of AIDS victims. They invited us out to their farm twice during our trip, and what I was struck by most was the juxtaposition of how things look to an outsider and how they are once you step inside.

On the surface, Watamu looked like a rougher, dirtier version of what I am used to. People dress similarly, everyone has a cell phone, we all buy the same things at the grocery store and as a tourist destination, there are nice resorts with all the amenities. Despite the similarities of the public face, things "behind the scenes" are more different than I supposed. And I'm still not sure how everyone keeps their cell phones charged.

As Priscilla and Japheth showed us around their farm in the next small town over, they talked about the cows and chickens they planned to buy to provide milk and eggs for themselves and their neighbors. As we ate lunch on the patio of their under-construction home, they talked about the $1,000US it was going to cost just to run an electricity line to their property. There is no "grid" per se to connect to, they were going to have to pay to bring it to them. And before we left on the 20-minute tuk-tuk ride back to town, I had to use the bathroom. They handed me a roll of toilet paper and pointed me off to a corrugated metal enclosure where I found a piece of wood with a handle covering a rectangular hole in the ground. These were Rotarians and business people, leaders in their community. And based on our first few meetings, I would have imagined their home life to look a lot more like mine than it turned out to.

Through Rotary, we also met Guido, the Italian owner of the resort where the local Rotary meetings were held and the President for the Club. We'd learned that Watamu was a popular travel destination for Italians and Guido spent three weeks of each month in Kenya and one at his apartment in suburban Rome. He'd asked for our help with brainstorming some ideas for fundraising around a scholarship fund the club was interested in starting. We agreed to meet up one Friday, and over a delicious Italian buffet and glasses of wine, we discussed ideas and plans for the scholarship fund as well as participation in a Kenya Red Cross shoe distribution that was coming up. When Guido learned we were planning to visit Rome, he insisted we stay at his apartment if our visit fell during the time he was not in town. We filed this invitation as well as his email address away for future use.

Two days later, in addition to a few other Rotarians, we had recruited some other staff and volunteers from Mwamba to join us at the local primary school to help distribute 10,000 pairs of TOMS shoes.

If you've ever bought a pair of shoes from TOMS, you know that they pledge a pair to be donated for each pair sold through their One for One program. They partner with local organizations, like the Kenya Red Cross, to do the actual distribution and with this model have distributed over 50 million pairs of shoes to people in more than 70 countries. TOMS' website says they send new pairs of shoes to their giving partners "who place the shoes directly on children's feet" and that is exactly what we did. Ten thousand students from all over the area converged on Gede primary school by car, tuk-tuk and foot to receive shoes. I promise you I saw 14 kids get out of one tuk-tuk, like no clown car I've ever seen.

We, as volunteers, spent the day literally putting shoes on feet. In addition to protecting children's feet from glass and other sharp debris, shoes in this area are critical protection from chiggers. I'd heard of chiggers, but thought of them as more of a nuisance than a danger. I was not aware that in dusty, less hygienic situations they are responsible for painful infestations that result in kids' not being able to walk and missing school. The provision of basic footwear is a huge deal to millions of kids worldwide. Getting to see this need firsthand made an impression.

In addition to connections made through Rotary in our "off" time, an entire month onsite at A Rocha allowed us to develop firsthand knowledge of the organization's programs.

One of the programs developed by A Rocha is called ASSETS. A combination of environmental conservation and community development, this creative program both meets the needs of the community and rallies local support for conservation by offering secondary school scholarships to families who agree not to exploit local natural resources.

In 2001, only 8% of kids who had the grades to go to secondary school (that's high school to Americans), actually attended. The main deterrent was a lack of money for school fees.

The area around Watamu is environmentally rich and because of that draws a good number of tourists. Within four miles of town, there are three intertwining conservation areas. The Watamu Marine Park & Reserve is a 4-square-mile area that protects marine and tidal habitats containing coral gardens just 330 yards off shore, 600 species of fish and 150 species of corals along with whale sharks, barracuda, octopus, manta rays and some important turtle nesting beaches. The Arabuko-Sokoke National Forest, less than 1 mile away, has 160 square miles of protected coastal forest, the largest and most intact of this type of ecosystem in East Africa. The forest is home to a large number of bird and butterfly species. It is also the only home of the endangered golden-rumped elephant shrew and the threatened Sokoke scops owl. Mida Creek is a huge tidal inlet with six species of mangrove trees that stretches from the ocean to the Arabuko-Sokoke. Covering 12 square miles, it is an important wintering site for migratory birds. Kenya has some of the best birding in the world, and the Mida Creek/Arabuko-Sokoke area tops the list in terms of seeing Kenya's rarest and most endangered species.

It's not uncommon for families living in and around these protected areas to illegally harvest timber, fish or bush meat to sell in order to raise the fees for their children's schooling. Although this might get a few children in school, in the long run it isn't sustainable for the environment or the local economy.

The ASSETS program uses money from tourism and puts it back into the community in the form of scholarships for families who agree not to engage in the illegal collection of resources.

The program also provides environmental education in the local schools and to the families of scholarship recipients explaining how the program works and why the resources are critical to the community.

Since tourism is the basis of funding for this key program, A Rocha is also deeply involved in developing and maintaining local tourism. This includes installations at Mida Creek and Gede, an archeological site where the ruins of a 13th century Arab settlement have been uncovered. We took the opportunity to visit both while we were in the area.

Mida Creek was a new ecosystem to me and one of the amazing things, besides the remarkable breadth of the mangrove forest, was the speed at which the tide rose. We'd heard much about the "boardwalk", and when we arrived what we saw was a series of sketchy swinging bridges suspended about 5 feet over dry sand. By the time we'd walked to the end, taken a few photos and returned, we were looking down at several feet of water. It was actually possible to watch as the water flowed in at a pretty astounding pace.

Along the boardwalk we were accompanied by young children, constantly running back and forth with their catch of small crabs – which they proceeded to eat, raw. At the end, we were treated to a view of the estuary and a parade of wooden canoes ferrying people back and forth from the far shore.

One afternoon near the end of our time in Kenya, I realized time was running out for me to visit Gede, so I jumped at the chance to join another A Rocha volunteer from the U.K. and a staffer from Kenya on a quick trip. Only a few miles outside Watamu, Gede is the site of a Swahili settlement established in the 13th century and inhabited through the 16th century by sailors and spice traders from Oman. It was a large Muslim community with around 2,500 people at its peak, composed of stone structures, including many houses, a large palace and grand mosque, all surrounded by forest.

Rediscovered and unearthed by the British in the 20th century, there is no written record of the town, unlike other similar Swahili settlements up and down the East African coast. The architectural style is definitively Middle Eastern and interesting to see against the much different post-colonial backdrop of modern East Africa. Besides walking through the village on interconnecting trails, there was a tree platform that afforded a unique aerial view.

Not only did I get to visit this impressive historic city, but I was also introduced to the wonders of the coconut on this trip. Now, I've eaten coconut, but I didn't realize there was a phase where the coconut flesh was so delicious and almost creamy. As the local expert, our A Rocha coworker insisted we pick up a few. We watched as the coconut seller skillfully macheteed the coconut open and carved a small utensil out of the husk. We thoroughly enjoyed every bite of coconut flesh while walking down the street using our little coconut spoons, and by the time we reached the main road to catch a tuk-tuk for the return ride to town, we tossed the empty husks and utensils off into the bush. No hassle, no trash, delicious snack.

29. LUMO Community Wildlife Sanctuary, Taita Taveta District, Kenya and wrap up in Watamu (Days 142 to 153)

About two weeks into our month in Kenya, I started to realize we'd actually be leaving Africa soon and we still hadn't seen a lion. For me this was not acceptable. We heard rumblings of another volunteer planning to rent a car and head inland a bit on safari and we arranged to tag along. Kenya is an expensive place for a safari, much more so than we'd found in South Africa or Zimbabwe. It seems like, at least in the U.S., Kenya is the go-to for African safaris. When you think of a safari, you most likely think Masai Mara, great wildebeest migration, etc., and so exorbitant prices follow.

Jean, our traveling companion, had amazingly managed to find a safari lodge with a campsite. We booked three nights in the camp and Jean worked on the car rental. It was a process to be sure.

Joseph, the "car guy," would show up at Mwamba with a car for us to consider. This one had no insurance papers, that one had no license plate, etc., etc. This process repeated itself, until the night before our journey at 8 p.m. when he showed up with yet another car that didn't meet criteria.

Finally, at 10 p.m., after multiple phone calls, he showed up with an SUV complete with a woman's purse still in the front seat and personal items everywhere. Apparently either the owner had been very anxious to earn some extra money, or Joseph had called in a favor and been very persuasive. This car didn't have current insurance papers either, but we were assured he would be at the office in Malindi (a larger town about an hour up the road) at 8 a.m. the next day when the insurance office opened to take care of it. We agreed, contingent on the papers, and paid a good bit of the rental fee up front. The next morning, we sat with our bags packed and half the bill already paid anxiously awaiting our newly insured car. Just after 9, Joseph showed up as promised and we were on the road in our "rental," now devoid of the presumed owner's personal effects.

We were headed to the LUMO Community Wildlife Sanctuary and the Lions Bluff Lodge, located 140 miles west of Mombasa. We'd experienced the route from Watamu to Mombasa on our way from the airport by taxi and it wasn't unreasonable – a two-lane highway with two-lane traffic. The drive from Mombasa west was another story. This section of the A109, or the Nairobi-Mombasa Road, provided the second-scariest day of our trip, close behind the water taxi in Guatemala. It was turning out that transportation was the scariest part of travel.

The Nairobi-Mombasa Road is primarily a two-lane highway over rolling hills. It's the only highway connecting the port city of Mombasa to the capital city of Nairobi and the landlocked nations of Uganda, South Sudan and Rwanda. Because of this it is packed with tractor-trailers carrying containers and loads of all kinds. Because it is a two lane road, traffic gets backed up by slow trucks on every hill, or it would if people had any hesitancy about passing a truck or three with oncoming traffic speeding toward them. Instead, it seems to be the norm to seize any break in traffic, no matter how small, and go for it, with the expectation that approaching traffic will pull over onto the shoulder if necessary, often at the last moment, to avoid a high-speed head-on collision. More often than not the approaching driver would slip back in between trucks just a fraction of a second before catastrophe, and I'd say only about one in 10 instances resulted in actually having to bail out onto the shoulder. It was like a four-hour-long game of chicken with vehicles far larger than us.

By the time we got off the highway in a town called Voi, I was exhausted from being sporadically terrified, my hand was cramped from gripping the door handle, and I was lightheaded from intermittently holding my breath – and I wasn't even driving. As we turned onto the dirt road leading to the conservancy, relief flooded over me and it was like the clouds parted and a chorus of angels started singing. We'd made it! As we entered the conservancy we were immediately encircled by a herd of impala, making the abrupt transition to tranquility shockingly complete.

LUMO is a relatively small wildlife conservation trust, located between the Tsavo East and Tsavo West National Parks. It's an important piece of land ecologically because it keeps the corridor between these two parks open for the flow of wildlife, and also educationally and economically because its structure as a trust benefits the local communities.

I wanted to see lions before we left Africa and this seemed like the place to come. The Tsavo area is known for its high density of lions; approximately 700 of the 2,000 lions thought to live in Kenya live here. These aren't just lions; these are legendary lions. Tsavo lion males are mane-less and have a reputation for aggression. The Tsavo area is famous for a pair of lions who killed and ate up to 135 railroad construction workers over a nine-month period in 1898. You may have seen the movie "The Ghost and the Darkness" starring Val Kilmer in the 1990s. Granted, this all happened a long time ago, but once an idea gets into my head, it's nearly impossible to force it to vacate completely.

We'd chosen the conservancy and Lions Bluff Lodge in particular because of its excellent Trip Advisor ratings and the fact that they had the rare and budget-friendly option of a permanent campsite. We'd been envisioning a campsite within maybe a few hundred meters of the lodge, where we could head to eat dinner or grab a drink. When we arrived, we found our camp rather more isolated than anticipated. From the hillside, there was an amazing expansive view of the valley. The lodge, however, wasn't even visible. In fact, it was a full 20-minute four-wheel drive trip away.

Our campsite consisted of two large canvas tents with (very comfortable) mattresses and bedding and a concrete block bathroom (in my mind, the lion-safe sanctuary). I immediately decided that we'd be going to bed, or at least retiring to read, rather early and that I'd be consuming no beverages anywhere near bedtime, because a midnight trip to the bathhouse was not an option for this girl.

Our first morning, we'd scheduled a safari drive. We figured we should get to looking for those lions ASAP in case it took a few days to locate some. This was an open reserve, where animals could come and go as they pleased, unlike our safari in South Africa, making it potentially much more difficult to locate the wildlife we were looking for. We drove around for a while, seeing some new antelope varieties, our first wild ostrich and a Kori Bustard, the largest bird capable of flight – but no lions. There was some chatter on the radio and conversation between our guide and others via radio, but since it was conveniently all in Swahili, we had no idea what, if anything, was going on. I was beginning to think we were on a bit of a wild goose chase and that my chances of seeing lions today had diminished to near zero when we turned a corner and there in front of us, not 15 feet off the road, were seven lions milling about and taking turns feasting on a buffalo carcass.

We had arrived just in time, and within minutes of our arrival the lions began to bed down one by one, sinking almost out of view and settling in for a long morning nap. For 10 or 15 minutes though, it was just us, our game driver, spotter and the lions.

Later that same evening we were able to follow some game vehicles from another lodge as they got a call from a game ranger about something presumably amazing and sped off. What we were rewarded with was a "binoculars-required" view of some occasionally visible lions on a distant ridge. In addition to being much farther away, this sighting was a sharp contrast to our peaceful morning lion viewing. We jockeyed for position with seven other game vehicles full of tourists for a spot to park, just to climb on the roof with the binoculars. Judging by the excitement of the guests in those other vehicles, I gathered that our morning sighting had been rather above average. I was even more pleased.

Along with the lions, we also happened across a serval (which, since our experience in South Africa, had become my favorite animal), and later in the day out tooling around on our own, we spotted a jackal and her handful of pint-size pups peering curiously out from the bushes at us. Priceless!

On one of our self-drive forays into the reserve, we discovered the luxury Sarova Salt Lick Game Lodge located on the far side of the reserve about a 45-minute drive over rough and remote dirt roads. (This is presumably where the other lion-viewers from the night before had come from.) The lodge itself had some pretty unique architecture. Each room is a rondavel on a pedestal connected by raised boardwalks all overlooking a watering hole.

The wildlife viewing was spectacular, particularly the elephant viewing. In addition to the watering hole, there is what amounts to a water trough at the edge of the main lodge building and an underground bunker in the center of the watering hole area that can be accessed by tunnel from the lodge. From this underground observation room, you get a close-up, ground-level view (through thick metal bars) of whatever wildlife has come for a drink.

The water trough is like a small moat separating the main hall of the lodge from the outside watering hole, just wide enough to prevent an elephant trunk from reaching out to grab anyone, but just barely. From this vantage point you could watch entire elephant families coming for a drink, including some of the youngest little ones we'd seen, up close and with nothing but air between us.

It was magical and I made sure we spent time every evening at Sarova communing with the elephants. Even though we were paying $40 a night to camp, there was no reason we couldn't share in some of the perks of the $250/night hotel "next door." Thrifty and resourceful, that's my motto. Oh, and always be friendly and act like you know what you're doing; that goes a long way too.

On our final morning, we packed our bags into the car for the (much-dreaded) five-hour drive back to Watamu. We'd been hearing hyenas rather close by each night and we got one final animal sighting surprise on the way down our campsite "driveway." As skittish and mostly nocturnal critters, hyenas can be difficult to spot, but we got a great view as they checked us out hesitantly from the bush.

Thankfully we survived the drive back, although in much the same high-stress fashion as our previous trek. At one point when we were almost back to Watamu we passed a police checkpoint. The officers had laid a tack strip across one lane, so we'd have to either stop or swerve into the oncoming lane to get through, and they were waving us over. We figured we'd been straying into the oncoming lane all day and on far sketchier roads than this. There was no traffic coming the other way and the officers didn't appear to have a vehicle in which to give chase, so we decided to decline their invitation to stop and continued home. I'm not sure what their reaction was as I chose to pretend everything was normal while continuing to look casually straight ahead. However, from the general degree of rule-following witnessed on this trip, I doubt they were incredibly surprised.

Every country we entered, one of the mental calculations I ran through was "Do I trust the police here? Do I think they are on my side?" The answer was rarely a certain yes, and mostly we just did our best to follow the rules, not do anything knowingly illegal, and to avoid all contact with law enforcement – sometimes you can't do all three and you have to choose.

Upon our return to Watamu and Mwamba, we had a few more days to finish up our volunteer projects, debrief with the program directors and take a final snorkeling trip before wrapping up with two nights at a resort down the street where we could relax, I could take a windsurfing lesson, and we could enjoy the last good night's sleep we'd have in Kenya, although we didn't know that yet.

Since we'd spent some extra money on our lion safari among other things, we decided that for our two nights in Mombasa we'd suck it up and stay at the Mombasa Backpackers hostel...in a dorm room. As much as I absolutely loved our time in Africa, we did not go out on a high note. I will now tell you unequivocally that I am too old to sleep in a hostel dorm room, but at the time I thought maybe I could squeak one more in.

The first night, there was a party that lasted until 3 a.m. We joined in for a while, made some friends, I even played my first ever game of beer pong. Around midnight, we put in our earplugs and attempted to go to sleep. We turned the lights off and the fan on in our too-warm room. It wasn't 10 minutes before someone came in, turned the lights on, used the bathroom, turned the fan off and left. Daryle got up, turned the lights off and the fan on. I am not kidding, this happened at least six times. Turning the light on, that part makes sense, it's part of sharing a room, but why every person without fail left the light on and turned the fan off when they left was completely incomprehensible to me. I'd also taken the very last bed in the room and the mosquito netting was attached oddly. Unlike all the other beds where the netting hung above the bed, allowing space between the occupant and the net, mine lay pretty much flat on top of me, making me hot, itchy and claustrophobic – not to mention failing to protect me from the majority of the mosquitos that could still land right on me and bite me through the net.

The second night was slightly quieter, but that was small consolation since we needed to meet our "taxi" (read: guy with car) at 3 a.m. to head back to the airport. We stayed in a lot of delightful hostels – in private rooms. We joke about the day we realized we were too old for hostels (meaning dorm rooms) a lot now. What was fine at 20 is not as enjoyable at 30 and downright unpleasant at 40. In the early morning, we greeted our driver, deposited our bags in the trunk and rode in darkness to the Mombasa airport, much as we'd arrived a month earlier.

And with that our African adventure was over. Although I was excited to head to Europe (and honestly, back to first-world comforts), I was also truly sad to be leaving such an amazing and exotic place. I'd loved the novelty of every day. I had wanted to visit Africa since I was about 10 years old and it had not disappointed but in fact over-delivered. I'd known people through the years who'd been to Africa for one reason or another and returned completely enamored. It seemed to be a permanent condition, one I now understood.

Although it was hard to leave, we'd been on the African continent for almost three months and there were other places to see. We'd decided to start our European adventure in the east and work our way west for logistical reasons. We were signed up for a travel blogging conference in Dublin (about as far west as you can get in Europe) in early October.

When we arrived at the Mombasa airport, we approached the check-in counter and were asked the standard questions.

"What is your final destination?"

"Riga," I replied.

"Where's that?"

"Latvia"

"Where's that?"

"Umm, northeastern Europe, near Russia," I offered.

Still no sign of recognition, but she dutifully typed Riga into the computer and came up with a tag for our luggage.

In hindsight, this exchange was a perfect metaphor for just how figuratively far apart Sub-Saharan Africa and Europe are and a foreshadowing of how different the next part of our journey would be.

Twenty-four hours later we woke up in what felt like a parallel universe.

Acknowledgements

I want to thank the dozens of friends and family who, in the year after we returned from what's become known as our epic vacation, heard our stories and asked if I was going to write a book – to which I confidently replied "no." If not for their persistent and repeated questioning, there would probably be no book at all.

Once I admitted that putting our experiences on paper was, in fact, something I wanted to do, I was the recipient of endless support from this fan club. "How's the book coming?" "When will it be done?" "Where can I buy a copy?" they would ask, making it impossible to quit.

Finally, nearly two years after first putting pen to paper and fingers to keyboard, there was a draft and I returned to that group for test readers. I am indebted to many for wading through that first draft, including Katie Huey, Vanessa Aschmann, Jamie Meyer, Mary Ericson and DeAnn Zamora.

I was relieved to see people enjoying my stories and took their suggestions to heart, both for a final edit of this book as well as for what needed to be included in "Part Two" which is now in progress and will cover the additional five months we spent in Europe, Morocco and Turkey.

I am indebted to Deanna at Lotus Designs for my cover design and Kindle formatting help, to children's author, and friend, Shari Schwarz for her encouragement and advice on "how to become a writer," and to Ashley Boothe and my amazing mother, Andrea Cacka, for a thorough edit of my final manuscript. Any mistakes remaining are most certainly my fault for not taking their advice.

Thank you to all the amazing people who opened their hearts and homes to us around the world. Without them, there would have been far fewer stories worth telling. And to my parents, Peter & Andrea, for encouraging my adventurous spirit over my formative first few decades and, when I announced this trip, for only asking once if I was really sure this was a good idea, before throwing in their support.

Last but not least, thank you to my husband, Daryle, without whom there would have been no trip and no book. I am incredibly thankful to have a partner in life who thought that selling everything and taking off was a great idea, happily spent 14 months on the road with me pretty much 24/7 and then was patient enough to help me wade through the learning process of turning those experiences into a format we could share. I'm blessed to have a husband who shares my belief that a life without adventure is no life at all.

I hope this book inspires others to pursue their dreams, to travel, and most of all to believe that anything is possible if you decide it must be so.

Happy travels,

Joyce Dickens, 2018

18863962R00219

Made in the USA
Lexington, KY
24 November 2018